EACH STEP
is the
JOURNEY

The Call of the Camino

Patricia A. Klinck

Kingsley
PUBLISHING

Published in Canada and the United States by Kingsley Publishing
www.kingsleypublishing.ca

All names except the author's have been changed. The places, events, and
dialogues are real and as remembered.

Cover and interior design and map: Dean Pickup
Front cover image: Dreamstime
Printed in Canada by Friesens
Distributed in North America by Alpine Book Peddlers, Canmore, Alberta
www.alpinebookpeddlers.ca

2013/1
First Edition
Also available as an ebook

Library and Archives Canada Cataloguing in Publication

Klinck, Patricia A., author
    Each step is the journey : the call of the Camino / Patricia
A. Klinck.

ISBN 978-1-926832-21-0 (pbk.)

    1. Klinck, Patricia A.—Travel—Spain—Camino Francés.
2. Camino Francés (Spain)—Description and travel. 3. Christian
pilgrims and pilgrimages—Spain—Camino Francés. I. Title.

DP285.K55 2013   914.6'11   C2013-903566-4

CONTENTS

FOREWORD

The Camino de Santiago de Compostela is a network of pathways that pilgrims have followed for more than one thousand years. They come from all over the world to Santiago, a medieval city in northern Spain—ninety kilometres from the Bay of Biscay and ninety kilometres from Finisterre on the Atlantic coast. Before the Christian era, ancient peoples held Finisterre, the mythical end of the world, to be sacred.

Santiago is named for the apostle St. James the Greater—later known as Matamoros, slayer of the Moors—whose bones are believed buried in the cathedral. Therefore, since the Christian era, pilgrims have believed they can bury their sins at the cathedral by doing a pilgrimage.

Over the centuries, Santiago and the pilgrimage routes developed importance for religious, economic, and political reasons. As rumours spread that the bones of St. James were entombed in the cathedral, the church seized the opportunity to extend its power and authority. It took over the protection and care of pilgrims and traders as a rationale for being there. Churches, convents, monasteries, and hospitals were built along the route. A university established in Santiago became a centre for learning and the arts.

The roads leading to Santiago became politically strategic. They were positioned to hold back the Moors who were pressing from the south and east, and the Franks who raided from the north. Increased population led to the growth of trade. Business flourished. The establishment of a mint signalled the area's economic importance.

Once over the Pyrenees, the Camino turns west and wends its way through parkland to the vineyards of Pamplona, then through the woods of Holm oak and on to Logroño, the city of Rioja wines. Just before Burgos is the archaeological site of Atapuerca where the bones of the first Europeans are located. León is on the *meseta*, a vast flat prairie. Then the route climbs through the Montes de León down to Galicia and finally to Santiago.

Pilgrims still walk the pilgrimage route and in increasing numbers.

They come on horseback, on bicycle, and on foot. They walk the entire route or portions of it according to time available and endurance. *Albergues* are traditional accommodation. Situated about every ten kilometres they support the daily walking rhythm. They are like hostels, with bunk beds, showers, and some minimal cooking facilities. Along the way are a variety of inns, restaurants, and markets where a wide selection of food—from sandwiches to meals—is available. For those who want more "luxury" there are small inns, *casas rurales*, and hotels.

But these are pragmatic notes for the reader. At its very essence the Camino is about identity. Common wisdom has it that we each walk our own Camino. Our perspectives are shaped by our genetics, by our experiences—and, yes—by our karma. The rhythm of one step after another for four to eight hours daily creates a space for thinking and a revised understanding of time. Time is related to space. Some people walk faster than others; some can keep a pace for only three or four days. Some slow their pace to walk with others. Most people opt to walk alone, joining others from time to time, but not feeling responsible for the other. We are alone in this journey, this life.

On the Camino, as in our daily lives, most of us expect that tomorrow will be easier, better, more. It might be. It might not be. We expect we'll get stronger as we walk. We might. But our weaknesses might weaken us even more. We come to recognize that today, this moment, might be the best there is.

Along the way we become aware that millions have travelled this Camino. We meet an array of people. They fall behind or move ahead of us. Some come back and some don't. Just as in life. Do we make those decisions? Do we choose? Are they part of our story that is given to us at birth?

As we walk, we come to see nature as our context: the brisk air of the mountains, the heat of the meseta, the humidity of Galicia. We live with landforms, vistas, vegetation, and birds. We stumble on rocky terrain, sink into soft grasses of natural paths, and slip on mud and cow pies. We revel in the clouds and the skies. We look into the eyes of local people and fellow pilgrims. We meet our inner self, the life-force, on the Camino.

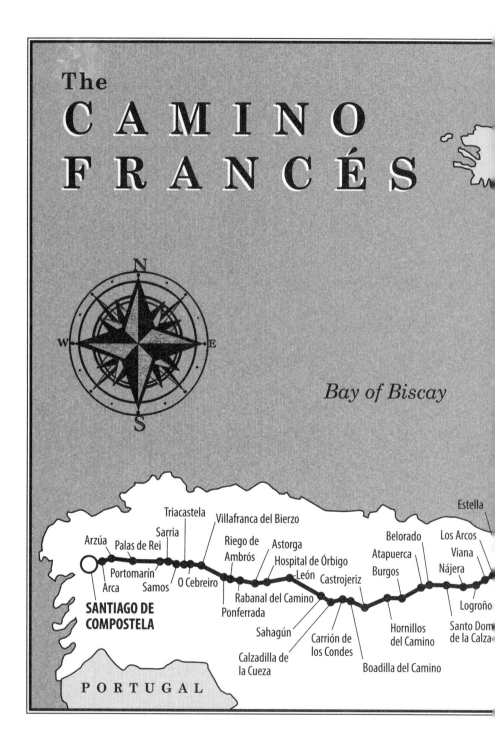

The
CAMINO
FRANCÉS

Bay of Biscay

Estella

Triacastela Villafranca del Bierzo

Sarria   Belorado   Los Arcos
Arzúa Palas de Rei   Riego de   Astorga   Atapuerca   Viana
                        Ambrós   Hospital de Órbigo   Nájera
       Portomarín   León Castrojeriz   Burgos
Arca   Samos O Cebreiro   Logroño
SANTIAGO DE   Rabanal del Camino   Santo Dom
COMPOSTELA   Ponferrada   Hornillos   de la Calza
                    Sahagún   Carrión de   del Camino
                              los Condes
              Calzadilla de   Boadilla del Camino
              la Cueza

PORTUGAL

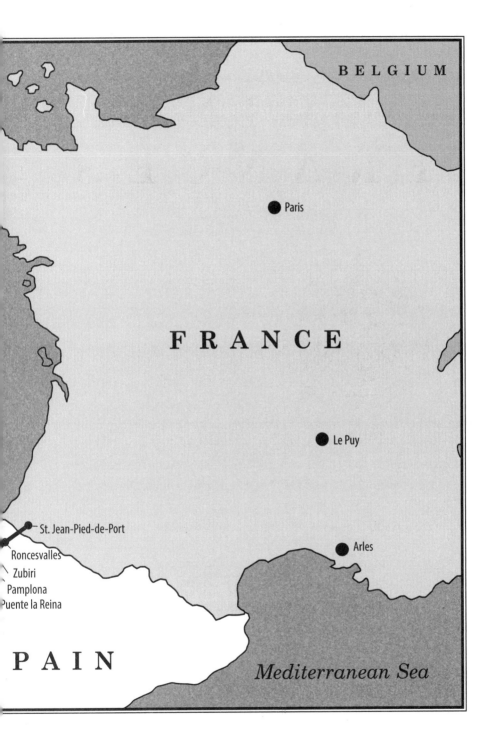

BELGIUM

● Paris

FRANCE

● Le Puy

St. Jean-Pied-de-Port

Roncesvalles

Zubiri

Pamplona

Puente la Reina

● Arles

PAIN

Mediterranean Sea

To my father, who lived his life with
infinite love and compassion.

———∞———

May the way be good for you.

CHAPTER 1

A SINGLE STEP

I wiped the fog from the window with my sleeve and saw the sign "St. Jean-Pied-de-Port" hanging from the roof edge as the train slowly ground to a halt. A gust of wind yanked at the hood of my anorak as I jumped down. Instinctively, I curled my back against the cold. Icy water splashed against my legs and trickled into my boots as I made a run for the station, my backpack slung heavily on my shoulder. If this foul weather continued, how could we possibly walk the eight hundred kilometres of the Camino?

There was the sound of the train door closing and Wendy and Mac running across the wet gravel behind me. We reached the station door together and burst into the empty waiting room. When no one showed up, I walked over and rang the bell at the main wicket. Eventually, a door opened at the back of the room and a woman appeared, pulling the door closed behind her. She wore a grey cardigan wrapped tightly around her body. I caught a brief glimpse of the room, a small radiator, and felt a brush of warm air. Her face was expressionless.

"Messieurs dames. Vous désirez?" She used the classic French greeting, her voice flat and hostile.

"L'Hôtel des Remparts," I replied.

She looked us up and down. "Pilgrims," she muttered. "Why don't you just look? There it is." She gestured through the window, turned, and left us standing in the middle of the station.

The rattle of raindrops and the slap of branches grew more insistent. We looked at each other. Wendy raised an eyebrow; I shrugged. Through the window we could just make out the hotel's neon sign. Someone had turned it on, but several letters were burnt out. Shutters blocked most of the hotel's lights and the short passageway leading to the main entrance was wet and covered with mud.

"Let's run for it," said Mac.

When we reached the hotel entrance we found the lobby in darkness. I shook off my rain jacket and wiped my face with the back of my hand. The hotelier stood up as we approached the reception desk.

"You are early," she said in French. "It is only eleven. You will have time to visit the Pilgrims' Centre to get your Camino *credencial* that is stamped each night. I hope the weather improves. They are saying it will clear this evening, but it is mid-September and anything can happen."

She pulled the registration forms from one of the pigeonholes behind the desk. The small lamp on the counter threw barely enough light to fill them out. She took two keys and passed them to Mac. "Everything should be in order. Please let me know if you need anything."

I looked at her; she would never even imagine what I needed.

Mac passed me a key and we trudged up to the second floor and found our rooms. "I'll come over once I'm unpacked," I said as I opened the door.

The room was dark, lit only by a shaft of light coming through partially closed shutters. When I opened the window and pushed out the shutters they rattled and the wind hit me with force. Outside I saw a low, stark white cloud moving against the hillside of autumn brown and yellow. Looks like snow, I thought, as I closed the window and turned on the lights. The guidebooks warned that with snow we might have dense fog. That would mean delaying our start.

The bed took up most of the space in the small room—its springs creaking ominously as I sat down and opened my pack. I pulled out my damp clothes and hung them out along the top of the dresser. It took no time at all. I've hardly anything in this pack, I realized. Wonder if it will be enough. Then I saw the black silk pants and dressy sandals that my friend Andrea had told me I must take. I remembered how serious she had been, her blue eyes drilling into mine.

"You have to treat this walk like a job. You start at the same time each morning— that way you have a ritual, something you can depend upon. You walk all day. In the evening you take a shower and change into your good clothes. Then, you find a table, order a beer, and start reading your book. Everyone'll be fascinated and come over to talk to you."

Good plan, Andrea, I thought. I'll start tomorrow. At the very idea my stomach knotted with anxiety. Tomorrow was day one and the longest day of the Camino: thirty-two kilometres and thirteen hundred metres elevation.

"Don't think about it. You've been on long treks before," I reminded myself.

I changed into a dry, long-sleeved t-shirt and headed for Wendy and Mac's room. "It's open, Pat," Wendy called out when I knocked.

When I pushed the door open they were sitting on the bed, close together. Clothes were piled haphazardly on the bed and the dresser. The room was warm and the storm seemed a long way from us.

"S-sorry," I stammered. "I'm interrupting."

"Come on in. You're not interrupting anything," said Mac. "Just sorting to see who carries what."

I sat down on the wooden chair. We looked at each other and grinned.

"So this is where it starts," Mac said.

"What's the saying?" I asked. "A journey of a thousand miles begins with a single step?"

"That's been around for a few thousand years, Pat," said Wendy. "Did you smell coffee as we came in? That's where I'm headed."

The sound of our boots on the wooden stairs echoed as we headed for the main floor. We sat at a table not far from people dressed in hiking boots and anoraks. Along the opposite wall were a buffet and a coffee machine. People were moving back and forth from their tables like automatons. Others were head down, absorbed in reading, and made no eye contact.

"Fellow travellers," I whispered to Wendy who nodded in agreement.

From where we were sitting I recognized the jacket covers of several of the books we had looked at last night. "See any books we haven't read?" I asked Wendy. She got up and reached for a bold red-and-white covered book on the top shelf.

"This looks new," she replied, thumbing through it. She stood quietly for several minutes. "Looks like it has some new approaches for managing the Camino experience. Think I'll get it."

"It will add weight," Mac cautioned as Wendy walked over to the till.

"What's on the agenda this afternoon?" Mac asked as he pulled a guidebook from his pocket. "I know we have to get our passports, buy makings for lunch tomorrow … Anything else?"

"That's after we walk around the town, see what it's like in spite of the weather, have a glass of wine …" I grinned at him. "You're seriously organizing us, Mac? It won't work!"

"He's a scope and sequence kind of guy. A real engineer, Pat," Wendy interrupted. "When we first got together, I was random, spontaneous, you know—like you are. But I've learned to appreciate it, and the other advantage is we don't argue anymore." She ran her hand over his hair. I grinned awkwardly and wrapped my sweater around my chilled arms.

We walked from the hotel to another bookstore on the opposite side of the street. It was wall to wall with pilgrims and the humid air smelled of their wet clothes. There were shelves covered with brochures, maps, and books on every aspect of the Camino.

"Nothing we don't already have," I said and turned to leave. It was then that I saw the sign: "Excess luggage—Roncesvalles shuttle."

"What's this?" I asked the clerk in French.

"It's very simple, madame," he replied. "Each morning we have a shuttle that takes excess baggage to Roncesvalles for ten euros. Guaranteed. Many pilgrims use this service. It is a long day and some things can go ahead. It lightens the pack."

"Wendy, Mac," I called out. "Just look at this! I'm going to send my sleeping bag ahead on the shuttle."

Mac looked at me. He was not smiling. "We haven't even started and you're already taking shortcuts. I thought we were going to walk the whole Camino?"

"It's my sleeping bag that is going in the shuttle. I'm walking," I retorted, hands on my hips.

"Well, not me. I'm carrying my entire pack. That's what the Camino is about—and life, too." His eyes were dark and serious.

I turned to Wendy who was looking at Mac. "What are you going to do, Wendy?"

She took her eyes off Mac and looked at me. "Not sure. I think I'll send some things on, too." Mac shrugged and we walked out, the decision hanging in the air.

We followed the steep, wet streets to the Pilgrims' Centre to get our credenciales. Each night along the pilgrimage, we'd been told that the *hospitalero* of a *refugio* or an *albergue* would stamp our credenciales so that, at the end, we would have evidence of each segment we'd walked.

As we approached, stomping our feet and shaking the rain off our hoods, a man opened the door. "Come in, come in! Quick! Such miserable weather," he said, his arms open to us. "Bonsoir. I'm François."

He was of average height, greying hair—an ordinary man, with a key to the rites of passage. His role was to hand out credenciales to pilgrims. He took my icy cold hands between his warm welcoming ones and I instantly clasped them closer. I told him in French that we were starting the Camino in the morning, just the three of us. He addressed me with "tu" immediately, which the French usually use only when they know a person well. Yet, with his soft demeanour, it felt right.

"Here are your credenciales," he said, holding them out to us. "Tomorrow morning you will find the Porte d'Espagne in the old town. That's where the Camino begins." Then he placed his hands on my shoulders and kissed me on both cheeks. "Just find the old gate, begin walking, look out for the *flechas*, you know, the yellow arrows, and embark on your pilgrimage." He smiled at us and added, "You do need one more thing. Choose a *coquille* for yourself."

The large wooden tub was full of scallop shells—the pilgrim's badge.

I looked down and let my hand hover slowly above them. I was drawn to one. It lay cupped easily in my hand, its fluted surface catching the light in its centre. The edges were slightly chipped and felt like broken fingernails. I turned the shell over, running my fingers along the outer surface. It evoked the sea. Poor little coquille St. Jacques, I thought. Plucked from its home to go across the mountains, then the *meseta*, to arrive in Galicia—perhaps to make it even to Western Canada! I felt warmth spread in me. This was such a fine start to our adventure. And my French was serving us well.

"What's the story of these scallop shells?" asked Mac, coming up behind me to choose one from the tub. "We're a long way from the ocean. How'd they get here?"

"You're right. They come from the shores of Galicia, which is covered with them. They remind pilgrims of St. James—St. Jacques, as the French call him—whose body was washed ashore miraculously covered with shells."

I rubbed my thumb along the grooves on the inside of the shell. "See how the grooves all end up in one spot? They say that it represents the ultimate goal, to reach the tomb of St. Jacques in Santiago de Compostela, our destination."

We found ourselves back outside in the fine rain. Wendy started, "Let's find a bottle of wine, some bread—"

"And thou singing beside me in the wilderness!" I interrupted. Our laughter felt warm and spontaneous.

"And," Wendy continued, "something to put on the bread." We climbed up to their room carrying a baguette, some cheese, and two bottles of wine.

"This is our first hotel picnic," Wendy commented. "There's no way, though, that we'll ever drink that much." The cork came out of the bottle with a "thunk."

"So," said Wendy, sitting on the bed, "let's review our goals. That's what the book suggests we focus on first." The bed sagged as Mac leaned back against the pillows. Wendy sat on his right. I perched on a chair near the bed.

"I just want to see what it's like to walk that far," Mac said. "I wonder if I can make it. I wonder how it'll go."

"No problem," I assured him. "It'll be really simple. First your left foot, and then slightly ahead of it, put your right foot, then the left …"

Wendy and I grinned at him.

"Easy for you to make fun," said Mac. "Just you wait!"

"Well, I want to explore the Camino as a metaphor," said Wendy. "I think that's what it's all about. A metaphor for living."

"Isn't it just straight living? After all, we are living and doing it—not just reflecting on it," I challenged.

"No," she insisted. "I see it from my point of view as a student of literature. Metaphors are important in understanding life. The Camino, walking this long voyage, is a metaphor for life. It will guide my thinking." She pursed her lips and made a note in her journal. "Your turn, Pat."

"I have three goals: to speak Spanish again, to see a part of Spain I've never been to, and to visit the cathedrals in Burgos and León, which I've read are real marvels of architecture." As I stated my goals I could hear the confidence in my voice; I believed in them.

"Is that all?" Mac looked disappointed. "I thought you, of all people, would have something else to say."

"I can feel there might be something else, but I don't think I'll know what until I have finished. I ju-just … " I began to stammer.

Wendy interrupted. "Surely you're not going to be that vague? Just think of all the projects you've planned in the past. These goals you're talking about are not strategic; they don't give direction. There's no bigger picture."

"Well … I sense there are parts of my life that I am not claiming as my own, that I am not fully resident in …" I looked down at my wine; I felt my cheeks flush. There was a silence. I twirled my glass, stuck for words.

Wendy came over to me and filled my glass. "That's just psychobabble," she said. "What are you trying to say?"

I looked at her and tried to explain. "Well, to use a metaphor, Wendy, imagine that your life is like a big, beautiful house. You have taken up residence in the house, but there are some rooms you've never seen, never entered. Those rooms, or realities if you like, are accessible—should you ever have the courage and imagination to open the doors and live in them."

Wendy ignored my comments. "Why don't we talk about the possibility of spirituality and the Camino? Everyone says the experience is spiritual."

I tasted the strong dark wine as it ran down my throat. The pungent smell of cheese filled the room. A sudden wind blew the shutters closed and I heard drops of rain on the roof. In my imagination the lights of the town and the distant sounds of people invaded our space. I wanted to walk away, leave this conversation, be somewhere else.

"Just what we need!" I exclaimed quickly. "More of the bad weather they talk about in the Pyrenees. Do you know sometimes it's so bad they can't even see the peaks? It's like walking the prairies. Well, I'm off! Six-thirty will come soon enough. Sleep tight!" I got up, stretched, and closed the door behind me.

• • •

I was lost. There were yellow arrows everywhere. They shone, changed shape, disappeared and reappeared behind me. I could make out an eerie glow in the distance. Then, just beyond the path, I saw a distorted, unrecognizable form coming toward me. It made a low, moaning sound. It wrapped around my ankles …

I awoke with a start. The light was coming in along the door jam and I could just make out the chair in the corner. I was sitting up, sweat running between my breasts.

What a terrible nightmare. So vivid. The luminous dial of the alarm showed three o'clock. I sank back into the pillows. My mouth was dry and I was restless. I groaned and tried to find a comfortable position, but the bed was hard and resisted my every move. Four more hours till we'd leave.

When sleep finally returned it was skinny and uneasy.

CHAPTER 2

BUEN CAMINO

It was six-thirty, and pitch black in the restaurant. Wendy and Mac joined me at seven. There was an eerie silence in the room. Several other groups sat drinking coffee and talking softly. Like us, they sported backpacks.

The three of us didn't say much to each other. Our excess baggage sat in an orange garbage bag by the door, ready for the taxi. How would we ever get that huge pile back into our packs, I wondered anxiously.

We found the trail quickly. It was seven-thirty, still dark and very quiet. Some people had left before us, but now there was no noise, no boots on cobblestones, no voices. It was as though we were the only ones walking this ancient pilgrimage. I felt chilled to the bone. My stomach was knotted and my breathing shallow. As I looked back I could see a few pilgrims still sitting in the warmth of the restaurant enjoying the smell of fresh coffee. The pack sat solidly on my back. I could feel the textured cork of the knob of my walking stick as I listened to the rhythm of my boots scrunching sharply on the gravel.

Ahead of me, Mac turned, his face ghostly in the darkness. "We're here." He pointed at the signpost. I ran my fingers along the chiselled letters: "Santiago de Compostela—790 kilometres."

"This is it," said Mac. "Let's do it."

I nodded but couldn't speak.

I remembered how quickly I had said "yes" to Wendy's invitation. And at each stage in the planning when I could have backed out, wanted to back out, I hadn't. I had not been able to escape the call; it had been so compelling. Now I was imagining the presence of all those pilgrims who, like me, had taken the first steps, felt the fear and kept on walking. I peered into the darkness.

Suddenly, from the deep shadows, two forms appeared. "Buen Camino," they intoned from deep in their hoods. Startled, I clutched my walking stick more tightly.

"What did they say?" asked Wendy.

"'Buen Camino' means 'may the way be good for you.' This Camino is the pilgrimage, the sacred way," I replied. "It is the greeting everyone uses as they meet other pilgrims."

Wendy and Mac started walking ahead of me. The outline of their shoulders melded to make one solid form. Wendy's head was tilted back and turned up toward Mac. The light caught part of her profile, her eyes deep in shadows. When I dropped in behind them I realized that the trail was wide enough for us to walk abreast. I moved to catch up, but they were already moving farther ahead and I knew I couldn't maintain their pace. The darkness circled around me and the silence deepened.

We continued walking, heading slowly through the thick, resistant night. I looked down, trying desperately to see loose stones and to gauge the steepness of the trail in the dark. My muscles were taut and the pant zippers rubbed against my thighs, the material hissing with each step.

Although the first part of the trail was a gradual climb, it soon changed and became a series of switchbacks. I was panting and I could feel a trickle of sweat down my back. I looked for Wendy and Mac, but they had disappeared ahead. We'd talked about this in Calgary and agreed on how we'd manage our different paces. Like all hikers we knew and respected the idea of pace. None of us was willing to change. We also knew and accepted that I'd often walk on my own. Yet, on this first morning, the logic of that decision escaped me.

I focused on my body and how it was responding to the challenge as the path steepened and the footing became more problematic in the darkness. My muscles seemed clumsy and ill coordinated. Experience had taught me this was the first stage of finding my pace and rhythm. Slowly, the muscles began to work together and my body warmed with the effort of climbing.

I turned and looked back to see the first rays of the sun shining over the foothills. The morning air stretched sensuously around me, the pack shifting subtly with each step. I am where I should be, I thought. This was the beginning of an adventure like no other I had ever attempted: the sheer distance, the varied landscape, the sense of a sacred and ancient path.

I stopped, zipped off the legs of my hiking pants, and began walking again, the air cool on my bare legs. The feeling of freedom was exhilarating. In front of me, the early morning sun explored the treetops and deepened the shadows at their base. The night sky had receded from inky blue black to a soft, iridescent lime green. As the clouds turned pink, rays of sunshine spread across the sky; the few stars flickered and went out. I felt warmth on my back and could see the way more clearly now.

The path was busy that morning. There were pilgrims walking in twos and threes, some chatting, others folded into deep silence as though meditating. For a while a man walked with me explaining the training program he had followed so that he could walk his best time daily. He was focused on how to do better each day.

"How about just enjoying the Camino, walking at your pace, smelling the roses, and talking with other pilgrims. Why not?" I asked tentatively. "Think about it. For centuries pilgrims have walked, ridden, covered the distance. Everyone says it's a pilgrimage to be enjoyed."

He looked at me, eyebrows raised. "I can't imagine how dull that would be," he replied. "If that was what I wanted I would have walked in the Yorkshire Dales where I live." He picked up his pace and soon left me far behind.

The countryside changed gradually from rolling hills to higher mountains. There were cows grazing in the grassy meadows, ponies tethered on the sides of hills, and sheep followed by shepherds and their dogs. At the pass I found Wendy and Mac again. I hugged them in the sheer pleasure of just seeing them so far from home. A large wrought iron cross marked the summit for pilgrims. Beside it was a small shrine. On the ground around the cross were pieces of paper held down by rocks. There were tiny packages tied to the rail fence around the shrine.

"Those are prayers from pilgrims," Wendy explained. "I was talking to a guy who is walking the Camino for the second time. He explained it to me."

I looked at the bright-coloured paper. "It reminds me of the medicine wheels on the prairies," I said. "Around those wheels are bundles for the gods, prayers in envelopes, and stones brought from far away. As offerings, I guess."

We stood silent and still. The mountain wind was strong and cool. Puffy clouds filled the sky and the sun was warm. Hawks circled lazily above us. I pulled an apple out of my pack and munched on it. The juice ran down my throat—sweet and cool. There had been no inns or stops on the morning's walk.

"Pat," Wendy called out, "come on over here." I walked toward the edge of the hill where Wendy, camera in hand, was reading out loud. "The Virgin of Orisson is just to our left. The guidebook says we should see her." I followed her reluctantly.

"This is just the first of so many statues of virgins. We'll see more than enough," I said to Mac. He grinned and nodded. But when I got there I saw a statue of a fragile, very young mother cradling her son. Her face was turned down toward him in loving adoration. It's the age-old story, I thought. The miracle of birth and the unconditional love of a mother caught here by some unknown sculptor and left on a wind- and snow-swept hillside. I looked around at the peaks and valleys. They would have chosen this spot because it's the highest—closest to God and visible to all travellers.

We moved off together talking about Spain and its mountain ranges. "It's the second most mountainous country after Switzerland," Mac announced. "The Pyrenees are just one of the ranges known for their beauty."

"Sounds like a photographer talking, not an engineer," I quipped. I looked around admiring the mountains but felt suddenly awkward and out of place—a foreigner. The Canadian Rockies were my landscape; I had explored them on foot, on horseback, and on skis. I knew them intimately through all the seasons. As I thought of them I could smell the air and see the evergreens—defiant wedges of black against the backdrop of moraine slopes—and the first snow-laden clouds.

I was soon walking on my own again. Wendy and Mac were ahead, talking with other pilgrims. Occasionally, there were bursts of laughter. This would become our pattern.

I found myself thinking of the way we met up in Heathrow. We had timed our arrivals close together. I had been a long way from feeling confident that we'd find each other even though Wendy had reassured me. My stomach had knotted as I walked into the packed customs area. What if I couldn't find their friend's apartment? How would I manage? I was watching the carousel for my backpack when I heard Mac's voice.

"You look like you're going on a pilgrimage," he stated, arms outstretched. "Shall we travel together? Have we met in a previous life?"

I had turned and hugged them both. "I've been thinking about how much longer the Camino would be on my own," I had said. I smiled at the memory.

The sun was higher in the sky and the pack poked at my back. I felt thankful for the cool, big wind that made the day so enjoyable. It smelled of pine trees, civilization, and faraway places. I leaned on my walking stick and was conscious of my lungs pulling deep. The path had become rocky and steeper. The backs of my legs were aching—a constant reminder of the effort of climbing. I looked up at the sky where traces of wispy clouds outlined the presence of the wind in the immense pale blue void. No birds. I revelled in the physicality of the walk, the trickle of perspiration between my breasts, the sound of my breath as I panted, the sun in my eyes. I thought again about my decision to come on this walk and how it had risen unbidden. Perhaps it came from my body and the deep, unspoken joy I had always felt in meeting physical challenges. Yes, in some sense my body had made this decision, recognizing its needs, knowing it would feel like this.

From a distance I could see a wooden fence at the top of the ridge I was following. The fence was built of hewn logs and as I came closer I could see their rough surfaces, dried and sunburnt. They were woven in a clumsy zigzag with dense bracken growing between them and along the fence line. I stopped, fascinated by the form and colour. As I walked over to the fence, my boots crunched in the bracken. The air was filled with its fragrance and the dry, sere smell of autumn. I ran my hand along the twisted top board. The surface was crisscrossed with gouges and deep lines. It rasped against my fingers as I caressed it. I stretched my hand along the top and wrapped my fingers around it. It was so thick. The trees used in making this fence had been giants—the products of time and the sky above them.

"Buen Camino," a man's voice called out. The moment was broken. I turned quickly, called back "Buen Camino," and hurried back to the path.

"Do you often check out fences?" he asked jokingly. He came up to me with great energy, swinging his walking staff, not breaking his stride.

"Nope," I replied. "But they caught my attention. I wonder how long they've been there."

He eyed the fence. "Well, about seventy maybe eighty years. They built their fences to last." We both fell silent.

"Well, I'm off—maybe I'll see you again somewhere." He lifted his hand and grinned at me. I watched him head down the trail and out of sight. A man in a hurry. There was no one on the trail ahead or behind me. I was on my own.

The village of St. Jean-Pied-de-Port was no longer visible. From somewhere came the deep, melancholic sound of bells chiming. They reminded me of François and the warmth of his embrace as he had welcomed us last night into the legions of pilgrims who have walked the Camino.

I had read in the guidebook that it had been the Celts, long before the birth of Christ, who first walked this path from south of Paris to the Atlantic coast. They had wanted to see the sun set in the ocean and miraculously rise again during the darkest point of the winter solstice. Their route—known

today as the Camino Francés—the French Camino—is the best known and
most walked of all the pilgrimage routes.

The Roman armies and the Christians came next. For each group and
every individual, there was a calling, a quest that could not be ignored or
denied. So they left their homes and security and followed the path that
led to danger, possible death, and salvation. Like each of us, they had their
reasons and their goals. In that sense, nothing had changed, I thought to
myself. We would live those experiences, too.

It was early afternoon as I came across a steep meadow of grass, lush
and green in the sunlight. In the middle of it stood several mountain
ponies, knee deep in the greenery. They raised their heads to stare at me,
their jaws rotating, their gaze speculative. I called out to them, "So, my
beauties, good food today, eh?" One of them wagged his ears and lowered
his head. Nothing was visible but his ears. I whistled as I would with my
own horses. No reaction. Even my whistle is foreign, I thought. I tried
again and called out to them. Their bells bonged with the rhythm of their
movements and echoed against a nearby mountain. I had stopped, leaning
on my walking stick. Suddenly, I heard laughter and looked up the slope.
Not far from me, part way up the slope, sat two women. I could just make
out the cadence of their voices and the occasional word. They grinned and
waved to me. I was sure they were French speaking.

"Hi there," I called out in French.

"Hi to you, too," came back the answer in English. "Don't you know
these horses don't speak English?" They pronounced it as "h-English."

"What part of Quebec are you from?" I persisted in French.

"We're not from Quebec," came the reply in French. "We're Acadians."

They got up and made their way slowly down toward me, following a
horse path through the bracken.

"I'm Maryse," said the taller of the two. "I'm from Moncton, Nouveau
Brunswick. And my friend here is Pierrette. She lives in Quebec City now."

"And I'm from Alberta—I'm Western Canadian, bilingual. We
represent Canada, east to west, right?" We nodded in agreement and
turned back to follow the path.

"You are interested in la francophonie, so I will give you a little test—okay?" Maryse was grinning with anticipation. Her dark eyes sparkled.

"Do you know that this is the four-hundredth-year celebration of Acadian settlement in North America?"

I felt my face turn red. "No, I hadn't paid attention to that."

"So what kind of Canadian are you?" She looked at me, not smiling.

"Try me," I challenged. "I know a fair amount about the Diaspora and Acadia."

"Well," said Maryse, "I was the head of the organizing committee for the last four years as we built up to the final preparations for this past summer. I've been travelling across the Maritimes and Quebec—even been out to the west a few times to do interviews, bring more publicity. And, of course, down to la Louisianne. There are so many connections still alive today, especially in the family names. They link all of us Acadians to our heritage." She didn't sound much like other Acadians I knew.

"Where is your accent from?" I asked, curiosity getting the better of me. Maryse turned to look at me.

"I was born in Saskatchewan; grew up in southern Alberta. We moved to Montreal, then Algeria for five years. I did my degrees in Paris when my father's company moved him again. So my accent is really mid-Atlantic."

"And you can hear in mine that I have spent some time in Quebec as well as in France, but mostly in Alberta?" We smiled at each other. "You know, when I think of accents, I think of identity. Without our accents we would be missing part of our passport. Why did you decide to walk the Camino?"

"I have always wanted to—for as long as I can remember. But I began planning it last year. I've been walking each day to get fit. Hervé, my husband, was not interested. He has his work, which is very important to him." I looked over at her. Her eyes were fixed straight ahead. There was a lull in our conversation. "I convinced Pierrette to come with me. As you see, we walk at very different paces." Pierrette had fallen behind us. I realized with surprise that she walked even more slowly than I did.

"Pierrette and I have something in common," I said. "We are both slower than our companions." I gestured to the empty path.

Last night, Wendy and Mac and I had talked about pace and how mine is slow. I told them once again not to worry about me being alone behind them. We'd just arrange where to meet in the evening. They still held out hope that we'd walk together. Today was day one and already that was not happening.

"Pierrette will leave the Camino in a few days and go back home. Then I will continue to the end by myself. I love walking this old Camino," she added. It sounded like a personal reminder.

I hesitated, then asked, "Do you feel a religious pull?"

Maryse chuckled. "Not much religion in me or in my family. We are too free-spirited to kowtow to a priest and a church. No, for me it is just something I wanted to do, badly. And this seemed to be the perfect time. I have finished my work. I don't have another job. No one is depending on me to be there. My children are at university." Her smile became radiant. "I have no responsibilities, no expectations but to enjoy each moment as it comes. To let myself walk, stop, enjoy the view." She gestured to the landscape and the clouds above us. "This is a perfect time in my life. I want to get to know more about myself at a rhythm that suits me." She laughed and whirled around to face Pierrette. "Come on!" she shouted. "It's time to celebrate!"

Then to me, she continued, "This is just like being a kid, walking out across the prairies. Once school finished, we spent whole days out there. No worries, no cares, no sense of time passing. That's me again."

I nodded to her and smiled. I knew the smell and the heat of a Saskatchewan summer.

I lost track of them that afternoon when we bumped into some other French-speaking pilgrims and they stopped to talk. I never saw them again.

The day grew hotter. I left the trail and headed for a shady spot and a flat boulder, then took off my pack and sat on the warm rock. I opened my water bottle, the water cool and refreshing. I lay back on the rock, folding my shirt under my head.

A spiralling hawk crossed my vision. He was following invisible pathways in the blue, head swivelling from left to right. His cry pierced the silence. He swung to the right, soared higher till I could no longer make him out. I sighed deeply and shut my eyes. The effect of the orange light inside my eyelids was soporific. There was the lazy buzz of bees nearby in the bracken. I stood up slowly and put the water bottle in my pack. As I picked it up, I heard the sound of the scallop shell scraping against the bottle.

Suddenly, the hawk plummeted to the ground, his speed controlled, his wings snapping out at the last minute as he grabbed a small animal. I saw him fight to gain altitude and then he was off, winging his way to the west.

It was late afternoon when I caught my first glimpse of the bell tower of the monastery at Roncesvalles. As I drew closer I saw Wendy and Mac at a small table, three beers in tall glasses in front of them.

"This one's for you, Pat," called Mac. "I didn't think you'd fuss about the brand." The sharp tang of the beer and its coldness slid down my throat.

"The perfect ending," I said, lifting my glass to them. "'Health, money, and love' or as the Spanish say, 'Salud, pesetas y amor.'"

"So what did you think, Pat? That was our hardest day according to the book." Mac looked relaxed.

"It was just another day of mountain hiking," I said with some relief. "The elevation gain—those thirteen hundred metres—didn't all happen on one ridge, so it wasn't as bad as I had anticipated. Maybe we should just chuck the guidebook."

Mac clasped it to him. "You can't do that," he said half-serious. "How will we know where to go?"

"Dead easy," I replied. "We are walking west to the Atlantic so the sun is always on our back; there are huge yellow flechas to mark the path. And also everyone we met today called out 'Buen Camino,' so they're fellow travellers and bound to help us. And the book does set up false expectations."

"Easy for you to say," Wendy piped up. "After all, you speak Spanish. Mac and I could always use our French but then …" She let it trail off.

There was a lull in the conversation as we sat in the sun. I undid my boots and liberated my feet from the unforgiving leather. I groaned with both pain and pleasure. Mac motioned to a waiter for a second round of beer. Wendy sat leaning back, her chair balanced, eyes closed, and her face turned up. Behind us the rays of the late afternoon sun softened the stones of the cathedral. The waiter approached with his tray of beer. Mac and I reached into our pocket at the same time.

"This one's mine, Mac," I said firmly, sorting my change.

"No, the next one is yours," he said, handing a bill to the waiter. "Are our rooms ready?" he asked. The waiter looked nonplussed. Mac looked at me.

"Are the rooms ready, señor?" I asked in Spanish.

"Yes, yes, señora," he replied. "You speak Spanish!" He smiled at me and at Mac who was popping the lid off the second beer.

"Mac shows the signs of a misspent youth, Pat," said Wendy, lazily squinting at me through one eye.

"Now for the serious business," said Mac. "We have to look at tomorrow and decide how far to walk."

I stared at him in disbelief. "Why don't we go visit the cathedral, hear mass being sung, and get our first blessing as pilgrims. We have a few minutes before it starts," I suggested.

Wendy's chair hit the ground. "Sounds good to me," she said. "Come on, Mac, leave your planning till later."

We walked into a twelfth-century church filled with light from the stained glass windows. Other pilgrims came in behind us, stopped to kneel, and crossed themselves before finding a place to sit. The chant of the monks resonated in the nave: deep strong voices of men singing with the conviction of their beliefs. Their red robes underlined their timeless presence; incense wafted over the pilgrims. I had often sat in Catholic churches where I had been deeply moved by the sound of Gregorian chant. Yet, this evening, in the context of this church, it took on new meaning. I could almost see hosts of pilgrims in the corners and shadows of the church. Their clothes were from centuries past, but the shells on their hats marked them as pilgrims walking on the trail to Santiago. I could pick out wounded men in army dress whom Roland had likely led into the fatal battle against the Basques. The legend told that on dark nights the sound of his horn was still heard in the valley. I could see them in my imagination: a pageant of people who had passed by here, who had lived and died in this place. I shivered. It was ages old, this Camino, and to be on it was to be in touch with its past, its present. So many others had lived and breathed it and so, I sensed, would we.

We left shortly after the blessing for pilgrims and went to Casa Sabina where we were to have our first pilgrims' menu. The tables were long and lined by wooden benches. The group was large, at least fifty people. There was energy in the hollow room where the noise of voices, plates and cutlery, and different languages reminded me of going to camp. The meal was simple fare as befitted pilgrims. It began with soup made of faded vegetables that had long since lost their flavour. Then followed the pasta and, in a chipped bowl, a tomato sauce with a meagre number of meatballs. Baskets of bread had been placed down the centre of the table. The service was simple: women from the town dressed in plain clothes. But the carafes of wine soon warmed the conversations.

Not long after the meal was over, I was rubbing my eyes, which were grainy with fatigue. It was hard to focus and my head seemed heavy. At that point another pilgrim came over and offered me a taste of a liqueur he said was made from blackberries. It went down my throat with burning haste.

"What in heaven's name is *that*?" I spluttered.

"That's Patxaran. It's local. Made in Navarre," he replied, looking amused.

I glanced over at Wendy and Mac.

"Well, that's finished me off," I said bravely. "What time are we meeting in the morning?"

Wendy set her jaw and said, "We need to leave earlier. Let's be on the trail by seven. The heat was bad today and tomorrow they tell me it will be worse—thirty-eight degrees." Mac and I looked at her.

"What was wrong with today?" I asked. "We got here in good time."

Wendy said nothing but looked at Mac and raised her eyebrows.

"Aw, I don't like early mornings, Wendy, as you know," his voice pleaded. "Let's be on the trail by eight."

"Good," I said quickly. "That's settled."

Wendy had the good grace to join in the laughter. As we started to leave the dining hall we heard someone calling, "Hey, you from Victoria? So are we!"

We turned and saw a tall, heavyset man with white hair and a beard walking hand in hand with a short, grey-haired woman.

"I'm David and this is my wife Marion. I saw your jacket," he gestured to Mac's navy jacket. "We're from Victoria, too."

"I think it's a different Victoria," said Mac. "We're from Victoria, a city in Canada. You sound like you might be from Victoria, Australia. This is my wife, Wendy, and our friend, Pat."

"Too right, mate," David said. "Big difference, but we're all doing the Camino."

I looked at the two couples. There was a palpable affinity between them. Wendy and Marion had started talking about how they had gotten in shape for the walk; the two men were moving back to the bar.

I said goodnight and walked up the stairs to my room. I washed slowly at the sink by the bed, looking in the mirror, which reflected back to me a white, tired face. I hope I'll sleep tonight, I thought. Last night had been fraught with such anxiety. I shivered. Where had those nightmares come from?

First day nerves, I thought. I'm so tired. I'll do better tonight.

—◦∞∞◦—

CHAPTER 3

MEDITATIONS

Wendy looked up, sleepy eyed. "Café au lait," she said, using her Calgary French. The waitress looked nonplussed. A slightly crazed look crossed Wendy's face as she realized she had spoken French. She snapped her fingers in the air, matador style, and shouted, "No, no … 'olé!'" The waitress spun on her heel and left the table abruptly. The three of us burst into laughter, spluttering coffee and juice everywhere.

As we arrived in front of our rooms, Wendy turned and looked pointedly at Mac. "Where will we stay tonight?" she asked. I said nothing, key in the door. It sounded as though she already had an answer. "Mac, and you, too, Pat, you both need to get rid of your middle-class hang-ups called privacy and privilege."

I heard the annoyance in my voice. "If we are really going to talk about this, let's sit down at least." I turned the key and shoved open my door. "We covered this ground in Calgary—several times. We agreed to stay in hotels and inns, not albergues. They are not up to our standards." Mac sat on the edge of my bed. Wendy stood up beside the night table, arms crossed.

"But now we're here. We've talked with other pilgrims who've stayed in refugios." Wendy turned to look at me. "They don't sound so bad, do they, Pat?" She raised her eyebrows and looked over at Mac.

Mac rested his elbows on his knees and sighed. "I hate the idea of refugios or albergues or whatever you call them. And I don't see why I should drop my middle-class privileges. I like my life like this."

"Albergue and refugio are interchangeable," I said calmly, then lost my temper. "But don't include me in your privileged middle class, Wendy," I snapped. "As for hostels, I've been there, done that. Once is more than enough."

Wendy looked surprised. "I don't remember you talking about staying in hostels. When did you do that?"

"When I lived in France. I was earning so little that we hitchhiked everywhere. Hostels were fine then. I was twenty-two and short of money. But not anymore. I still tent in the backcountry; otherwise I stay in hotels. You know I brought my sleeping bag in case we ran out of options. But I prefer not to stay in albergues." I exaggerated my Spanish pronunciation.

Mac tossed his head back and laughed. I felt my face grow hot. Why had I been so dogmatic? Such a snob! Embarrassed, I laughed, too.

"Yeah, you stay in an albergue if you want to, Wendy," he said. "We'll meet you for breakfast." Mac turned toward me. "I am amazed that you, of all people, have hitchhiked. I think of you as ..." he paused. "Well, it's not your style."

"I loved it," I said. "One morning, back in Edmonton, I passed a guy hitchhiking on my way to work. I wanted, more than anything, to stop and change places with him. To be free, self-sufficient, with everything I needed on my back, heading off with no agenda. That's really my style, Mac."

"So," Wendy looked at me, a challenge in her voice, "why not have an adventure staying in an albergue? That breaks the pattern, opens up ways to meet other people."

"I've got to admit it sounds better when you call it an 'albergue,' Wendy. But it doesn't change the smell: old, unwashed, too many unclean bodies, cracked, dirty linoleum ..." I paused.

"You've convinced me," said Mac.

I looked at Wendy. She met my eye but said nothing.

"We likely won't ever do this walk again, Wendy, and I know you want the experience of staying in an albergue or whatever," I continued, "so you two could buy sleeping bags and give it a try if you really want to. If worst came to worst I would join you. Or, of course, I could just meet you for breakfast."

Mac nodded. "Let's give it a miss," he said as he stood up from the bed and looked outside. We could see the soft pink yet bright sky through the double windows.

They headed back to their room. I picked up my pack and balanced it on my knee. Before leaving home I had weighed each item, determined to keep the weight around ten kilos. Yesterday, when the orange plastic bag filled with my excess arrived, I was shocked once again at how much there was. I punched the sleeping bag in on top and stuffed the extra clothes along the side, then set the pack on the floor. It rolled over drunkenly. The top flap was pulled tight and strained against the shoulder straps. The only other way to manage it was to mail the excess home. An expensive proposition.

There was a knock at my door.

"Coming," I called out as I heaved the pack onto my back. Day two was about to begin.

We started up the trail together, Mac leading the way, Wendy directly behind him, and me following at a short distance. I thought about the talks we had before leaving Canada. But now we were on the Camino. We had talked with other pilgrims and locals, seen the countryside, and were about to walk our second day of more than twenty kilometres. Other issues would come up and decisions taken in Calgary would be revisited. All that made sense. Ahead of me Wendy's tall slender body walked with a measured gait. Her enthusiasm was infectious. I trusted that as long as we talked openly we'd figure things out. I looked up to see them disappearing around a bend.

The sun shimmered; the silence hung suspended. There was a feeling of space, which stretched out from the valley where I was walking to the mountains on either side. It was hauntingly familiar. Somewhere at sometime I had walked in a mountain valley with a similar vista. The path climbed, turning to the left, and then I remembered. It was in France, in the gorges of the Tarn. As I walked on I remembered the beautiful and uninhabited countryside there. I had signed up for a five-day, self-guided walk, confident there would be others on the path and that I would join up with them—maybe for a meal, maybe to walk a ways together. When the voice on the other end of the phone told me I was the only one walking and that he had already processed my VISA, my heart sank. To be so alone, possibly lost, in that rugged area of France had been daunting. Well, I thought, at least here I'm not alone. I looked around again. There was no sign of a village or a farm. The old sense of anxiety flared and my stomach knotted. I shrugged off the feeling. If it were like yesterday, pilgrims would be spread out along the path and sooner or later someone would come by. Meanwhile, I'd enjoy this gift, this beautiful morning. I deepened my breathing till it became soft and easy. Here I am, I thought, alive right here and now, right in this moment. I raised my arms and saluted the peaks and the sky. I smiled to myself and watched my boots swing in and out of my vision.

The path climbed slowly and my feet moved along the stony trail with greater confidence. My legs were pink from the warm sun of the high country. My walking stick tapped out the rhythm, the metal tip hitting rocks then soil then rocks. Its tapping lulled my anxiety.

Just then a voice behind me said, "Buen Camino." Startled, I whipped around to find myself eye to eye with a short, stocky Asian man. He was wearing the kind of bamboo hat I associated with rice paddies. His grin was infectious.

"Buen Camino," I replied. He bowed and I bobbed my head. We both laughed as he passed me.

The path followed the contour of the hills, dropping down abruptly at times and pulling itself back from creeks and boulders. It was heavily wooded and I breathed in air fragrant with the scent of pines. These were the foothills of the Pyrenees.

It was nearing mid-morning and the sun was intense. As I walked into a small café, I saw the headlines of a newspaper: "Unseasonably hot weather for northern Spain. Temperatures of 38 to 40." No wonder it's such hard going, I thought to myself as I ran my fingers through my damp hair. I must be even slower today than yesterday. Again, I felt an unwelcome flicker of anxiety.

I ordered iced water. The condensation formed drops of water around the base of the glass. I remembered Paulo Coelho's book *The Pilgrimage* about his walk on the Camino. He had an invisible, spiritual guide who travelled with him and who recommended that he perform daily meditations. He could choose from several possibilities. One involved making patterns in the condensed drops of cold water at the base of a glass. Absent-mindedly, I put my finger in the drops and spread the moisture across the table. Abstract patterns and connections began to appear. Lines I'd made from the drops of water formed a blob, which had connections to other shapes. Some lines simply wandered across the dark brown wood. I shook my hand and droplets fell at random. I squinted at the whirls and shapes. Some looked like profiles, perhaps of pilgrims who had walked the Camino over the centuries. As I had walked alone that morning, I had focused on stories of the Camino, its pilgrims and its history, events, and pageants. I had imagined the Celts in their mystic rituals of death, returning from the ocean as the sun rose above the horizon. And I had revisited the church at Roncesvalles in an earlier time, saw its priests in red robes intoning Gregorian chants as they walked in among the prostrate pilgrims. I could smell the incense, imagine their lives. It was all so real. I could step off this trail and enter any of the worlds I felt and saw around me. Now, as I looked at my finger art, the patterns began to fade and the waiter's voice broke the spell.

"Something else, señora?" he asked. I smiled at him, stood up, and opened my wallet.

I looked around the room. Several men were playing cards; others were staring into space. Noiselessly, the memory of the first night's dream came back. My confidence buckled and I saw my face in the mirror behind the bar. My eyes were vacant with anxiety and a cold sense of foreboding occupied my body. I shook myself. Enough of this, I thought. I paid the bill and walked out into the blinding white light. When I met Wendy and Mac in Zubiri I'd talk to them about these visions and we'd have a laugh.

The path had begun to climb again, the trees getting thicker. At one point, I walked past a large shed with a white cow lying in it. She rested between her calf, which was stretched out along the wall, and me. She lowed softly when she saw me. I stopped and spoke to her, crooning my admiration for the calf. Her head swung from side to side as her apprehension grew.

"No problem, old girl," I crooned again. "He's safe. I'm not going anywhere near him." She began to heave herself up, her front legs propped up in front of her. I picked up my pace, leaving her before she stood up completely. The look in her big brown eyes was soft and protective. It was almost a nativity scene, enveloping love, protection—a mother's mandate. I thought of the Virgin of Orisson we had seen yesterday, a simple statue but alive with compelling humanity.

By one o'clock I was famished. I walked into a small square and past an open window. In the shadows behind the bar, I saw the white apron of a barmaid.

"How's it going?" I asked as I entered.

She smiled. "Too hot," she said, wiping her neck with a handkerchief. "What would you like to eat? Drink?

I ordered a sandwich just as two people filled the open window. Mac and Wendy. My heart soared.

"What a surprise!" I said. "I'm so glad to see you. Let's have a coffee together. When did I pass you?"

"Nope," said Mac. "We are way behind time." Wendy had an eager look as she turned away from the window.

"No problem," I said. "Go ahead. I'll see you in Zubiri." I turned to chat with the barmaid, finished my coffee, and left. As I stepped outside, the heat was like a white barrier. I walked close to the walls of buildings where there was some shade. My feelings were dark, formless, inchoate. I couldn't deny them. I walked on in the heat.

As I trudged on, walking more slowly, I tried to name the feelings, to let them go, but they hung on. I struggled with the idea of saying something to Mac and Wendy but decided against it. How could I say anything, I wondered, when I didn't know what was bothering me. After all, I had often walked on my own. That wasn't the problem. We had talked about our different paces before leaving. And besides, there was no reason they should stay with me. Their sense of urgency was much stronger than mine so it made sense for them to go on ahead. I had encouraged them to leave. I found myself stopped near a bridge. I looked around in embarrassment. Thank God there was no one to see me standing here like an idiot. I picked up my pace, swung my stick, and changed my thoughts.

I arrived at Zubiri at the end of the afternoon, tired and hot. As I neared the river I saw Mac and Wendy walking toward me.

"Hail, pilgrim," Wendy called out. "We've found a small hotel and booked it for the night."

"You're great, you two. But one more question—have you ordered a beer?" We laughed and Wendy and I exchanged a hug.

It was near six when we headed into the centre of town and the Internet café. We sought out one of the pilgrims' restaurants, which opened earlier than the ones catering to the Spanish, who like their evening meals around ten-thirty. We walked along together barely talking of our day. Our fatigue groaned in our legs and our stomachs were empty.

As we climbed the stairs, we were met with the sounds of voices, other languages, the smell of food and beer. The room was long and narrow. A table, covered with a green cloth, ran its length. People were sitting in front of place settings on both sides. The table was nearly full, but we managed to squeeze in beside three men.

"Good evening. How's it going?" queried one of them. "I'm Geoff, from Tucson. I've been on the Camino for three days. These guys are Helmut and Franz from Germany. We walked together today."

The one nearest me extended his hand. "Ja, so I'm Franz," he said, his ruddy face solemn and his handshake firm. "Wir sind deutsch," he said in

German, then startled, corrected himself: "We're German, Helmut and me."

Helmut smiled shyly. His eyes darted from Franz to Geoff. "Good evening," he said quietly and shook hands. "We are walking now for two days."

Mac joined in quickly. "We started out at St. Jean-Pied-de-Port and this is our second day, too. Great day today—and yesterday, too," he hastened to add.

Wendy lifted her glass. "Here's to walking the Camino." They both smiled at the men. Helmut and Franz lifted their glasses in unison. Geoff turned to look at them, then raised his glass. "Good luck," he added.

The waiter came swinging into the room, the bar doors slamming behind him. He wielded the loaded tray with finesse, calling out: *¿Sopa? ¿Ensalada? ¿Bistec?* Conversation slowed as people quickly raised their hands to make their choice. The first course was plain macaroni without sauce, but it tasted like gourmet food. I was starved. I looked up at my companions: their eyes lowered, a look of intensity on their faces.

"'Hunger is a great host.' That's what we say in my family," I grinned at them.

Mac slowed down and said, "The first bite is the best—literally." Geoff joined in our laughter.

Franz scowled. "So what is it? What did you say?"

"Oh, just an old American saying. Hard to translate," Geoff explained.

"Not really American," I contradicted him. "We're Canadian."

He shrugged. "So what's the difference?"

It was my turn to shrug. "We'll talk about that some day, Geoff," I offered as I closed the conversation.

"Are you assuming we'll see each other every day? This is the Camino, you know. There are thousands who walk it—all at their own pace. These guys are my second lot of companions. The first guy I walked with I left behind this morning. We were talked out. Nothing left to say. Likely never see him again. And that's fine with me. You can only walk for so long with one person." He picked up his glass of wine.

I flinched at the indifference and judgment in his voice. "So the Canadian-American differences will go unclaimed," I said with a smile. "What's for dessert, Wendy? Does it fit into our calorie count?"

"Your wife is on a diet? This must be Canadian men!" said Helmut. "In Germany she is very—how do you say it—small?" His accent was strong and he blushed a deep red.

Wendy looked at Mac and retorted, "It's what Canadian women think is good that counts!"

"Yes," I added. "Their opinion counts but who's counting?" We all laughed.

"How do you find walking each day?" Franz asked. "We are German. We walk every day a very lot." He fixed his solemn gaze on the French hikers at the end of the table.

"It's not a question of your country of origin," snapped the French man. "It's got to do with the health of the individual—age and stage are of no importance." The talk became more animated. People switched from French, English, and German—the laughter was easy.

Then, in the middle of the talk and laughter, the desire to cry—to just sob out loud—overwhelmed me. The feelings were the same as when I was a child: cold, a crunchy feeling in my palms, twisting in my gut, a sense of non-reality, buzzing in the ears. It had been years since I had felt like this. Why now? What has a pilgrimage got to do with childhood trauma? Where did that feeling come from? It felt terribly familiar.

I realized that my shoulders had hunched over, my head was in my hands, tears stood in my eyes. The memory of a night long ago when my parents had rushed to my bedroom to calm my incoherent sobs came to me. The darkness, clammy hands, the nameless fear, the sense of doom were still buried deep inside. I shivered involuntarily. Through the blur of tears, I heard a French voice, "Eh, bien, Patricia … what do you think about that?"

What was the question? I chastised myself and tried to laugh along with them. The joke was at my expense. From the end of the table, one of the French asked if Canadian women were all so sensitive. Mac assured them it was rare. No more of those feelings, I whispered to myself. Embarrassment flowed through me.

The talk turned to discos and bars in the small town. Someone announced suddenly that it was nine o'clock. At that we got up and headed for the door.

"Well," said Geoff, "I think I'll follow the Canucks and get some sleep." We followed him to the front of the restaurant, saying our goodbyes to Helmut and Franz.

Bed felt so good that night. The sheets were clean and pressed. The towels threadbare and the pillow thin, but that hardly mattered. I splashed warm water on my face, luxuriating in the silence, the privacy of the room, and the sheer fatigue of walking fifty-five kilometres in two days.

CHAPTER 4

ALONE

It was well after eight when we left the hotel. Neither Mac nor I had wanted to leave in the black of pre-dawn. I loved the moment of anticipation as we stepped out onto the path to greet the soft pink of morning. I didn't want to compromise and follow a regime, leaving at a certain time, stopping for lunch at a certain time. I wanted to "be" on the Camino, not "do" the Camino.

The sky brightened and golden light shot through it. We were headed for Pamplona some twenty-five kilometres away. As I walked along I realized how tough yesterday had been emotionally. It's only the third day, I thought, as I watched Mac's red jacket and swinging stick heading down the valley in front of me. He walked with obvious rhythm and feeling for the day. Well, that was his goal—to see if he could walk it all. Behind him was Wendy, lithe and alert. I felt affection reach out from the bottom of my heart and enfold them. At breakfast that morning, Wendy had said again, "He likes to plan. So that's how we travel: destinations known, stops scoped out, and exact time for eating each day. Tested over twenty years— and presto! It works." We had both laughed.

It's a big change to travel with a couple, I admitted to myself. Mac is more task-oriented than I am. They are so used to each other. And I am so used to being on my own. I didn't feel like changing my focus, my timing, my rhythm, and neither did they. I listened to the tap of the walking stick. Not a bad pace, really. Not going to eat up miles, but it had always gotten me to my destination.

The sky had turned brilliant blue and the sun was making personal taps on my back. I looked down at the familiar sight of my walking stick keeping in rhythm with each stride and realized that I loved the pace and that it would strengthen me as time went on.

An hour later we arrived together in front of a small coffee shop. "Café con leche?" Wendy asked. We stopped, had our coffee, and then the focused walking started. Soon Wendy and Mac were well ahead of me. I walked on in the aura of the conversations of the last days. I turned them around in my mind the way I might turn a kaleidoscope to see the different patterns.

As I crossed the plaza of Larrasoaña, I spotted a small church on a side street. I pushed open the door and discovered a cool, dark interior with a spot of colour where the sunlight streamed through the stained glass window. The smell of incense was strong. In the front pew sat an old woman, rosary in hand, eyes shut. As I sat down a feeling of calm and peace rolled through me.

It was around ten o'clock when I left the church. The sun was high in the sky; the heat was building. I walked slowly across the plaza and picked up the yellow arrow for Pamplona. The gravel road turned to the west, passed under some trees, and headed across the open land. As I left the town, a dog got up and slid over into some shade. He dropped down, stretched out his neck, and eyed me calmly. I shifted the pack slightly and walked a bit faster. There was no one else on the road. The sense of silence, the heat, and the parched fields were strangely welcoming. In the core of my body I could sense a warm centre. It rose and fell in my breast like butter, soft, yielding, and golden. Its calm stretched out and all thought left. My stick tapped out a rhythm on the stones.

The next sign for Pamplona brought back a host of memories. It was Hemingway's city. He had loved bullfights and the San Fermín spectacle of the running of the bulls through narrow, crowded streets. A lot of what

I knew came from reading his books but even more from going to my first bullfight there. It had been in early August and hot. I was studying Spanish in Jaca, about an hour from Pamplona, and had never seen a bullfight. Several of us drove over with one of the profs. The crowd was huge, the wine harsh, the sun punishing. To my amazement the crowds shouted "olé" for the courage and skills of the bull or the matador! The bulls were enormous, terrifying in their unbridled aggression. I left that day an amateur of the ancient ritual.

Along the road were small crosses built by other pilgrims. I stopped and looked more closely. The stones were piled one on another; some were the red of the fields, others dun brown, some were crisscrossed with white lines like tracery. A twig or a branch formed a cross in others. I noticed pieces of paper sticking out. As I bent down to pick one up a sense of trespassing overwhelmed me. Whatever the conversation—and whomever they were talking to—it was private. It would be an intrusion to read it. These were pilgrims' silent pleas for help, for succour. I made sure the note was well tucked under the cross. The sides of the road grew steeper and the crosses soon disappeared. The sky was a light blue, no clouds.

I was nearing the top of a ridge when I heard voices: children's voices, the first I had heard in more than two days of walking. The only children I'd noticed were in towns. This was rugged, isolated countryside. I picked up my pace. In the flat area below the ridge were picnic tables and a playground. Two women were there with their children. The little girl was on a swing, with her mother behind her, pushing her and calling out words of encouragement. I stopped and watched as the girl leaned back and stretched her feet to the sky.

Two boys were playing on the nearby teeter-totter. As I watched, the bigger of the two began to bounce the plank. I had a vivid memory of my father doing just that. I had been helpless to stop him. His laughter still rang in my ears. I heard fear in the voice of the smaller boy as he lost his balance. His tormenter continued laughing. Another woman ran from the picnic shelter toward them. Just as she arrived the little boy fell off and began crying. She picked him up, brushed him off, and inspected his knee. The older boy stood just behind her, hands behind his back. She turned to him, scolding him, pointing at the teeter-totter. She grabbed the boys' hands and they went into the shelter with the picnic table. At that moment, one of the women looked up at me and waved. I waved back and started along the ridge. As I left the playground area, I glanced back and noticed they were putting the children in a car and preparing to leave. I wondered where they lived; I hadn't seen any farms or houses since leaving the village.

The afternoon heat defied movement. Each ray of the sun became an attack on my being. The silence was oppressive and the air hung motionless. The crunch of my boots and the tap-tap of the stick were the only sounds. Suddenly, a man walked by me. I turned to him.

"Buen Camino," I said, one pilgrim to another. He remained silent and didn't make eye contact. He was dressed in workmen's blue trousers and jacket, his hat pulled low on his head. He had no pack and I wondered idly where he came from since he wasn't a pilgrim. There must have been a house in the distance. The path ahead of me followed the contours of the ridge and he soon disappeared from sight.

It was at the next turn that I saw him again. He was leaning back against the bank near some trees. His pants were dropped down around his ankles and he was holding his penis in front of him, moving his hand up and down agitatedly. In spite of the heat, I was instantly cold. My mind scrambled frantically. His penis was flaccid and bobbled as he waved it. Were exhibitionists violent? Were impotent men likely to attack? How long was it since the playground? Fear quickened my heart rate. Sweat broke out under my arms. I didn't break my pace. I grabbed the walking stick below the knob, balancing it in my hand. I remembered being told that women don't tend to go for the eyes or the penis, areas of vulnerability. I knew where I would strike. What if he didn't attack as I walked by? What if he followed me? The trail was narrow, barely a metre across. I would be so close to him as I walked by.

Would he attack me as I approached? Or would he hit me from behind? I kept on walking. All of a sudden I realized I had passed him. I was on the other side, still walking down the path. The silence deepened. I could hear the sound of my breathing, shallow and rapid. I could not remember seeing the man as I had passed by him. I couldn't recall his face, what he looked like. Was he dark haired? I had no idea. Nothing. No memory of him. Did he say anything? No, I thought. He had been wordless.

The trail turned to the left. I found my pace again and turned to look over my shoulder. The path was empty. It meandered along the middle of the ridge. I looked back again. No one. I began to walk faster. Maybe he wasn't following me. Maybe exposing himself was enough. The trail bent to the right, climbing steeply. I looked back again and there he was. He was swinging his jacket over his shoulder, naked torso, striding down into the valley. Even at a distance I could see how big he was, the bulge of his hips, the slope of his shoulders. His hat was pushed back on his head. He walked quickly, with a sense of purpose. My shoulders dropped. Thank God.

The emptiness of the fields floated around me. I saw several hawks circling above, looking for food. The bushes were dried out, the thistles skeletal. I tried to gather my scattered reality. Nothing happened, I reminded myself. You are safe. He isn't coming after you. The moments of the day have been beautiful. Now is beautiful. Stay with the gift of the walk. Watch the shadows. Think of the patterns.

My heart slowed down, the thumping quieted. On the horizon, I made out the outline of the next church and the huddled buildings surrounding it. Time for coffee and some conversation. As the details of roofs and doors became clearer a sense of urgency overwhelmed me. Yes, coffee and some talk, some company.

There were only a few people in the coffee shop. None were pilgrims. When I opened the door, those inside turned to me and smiled. My heart surged. I smiled back.

"How is the pilgrimage going?" one of them asked in Spanish. "Do you like the walk? Where are your companions? Are you alone?"

Their interest shone in their eyes. I told them I was Canadian, from the Rocky Mountains, that I loved Spain, its people, and their language. They nodded and told me that my Spanish was very good. We tilted our coffee cups in celebration of Hispano-Canadian relations. The smell of coffee, their dark eyes, and the sound of warm voices stayed with me for the rest of the afternoon.

I arrived on the outskirts of Pamplona at about five-thirty, followed the flechas and finally a sign pointing to the plaza. Mac and Wendy were sitting under the awning of a bar with another couple. I left the shade of the buildings and began to walk toward them. There was dead silence in the plaza, no movement, windows shuttered. The heat and glare of the sun were physical presences. The distance between my friends and me seemed to lengthen as I moved across the open, empty space. I walked on, heard each footfall, felt the pack hanging like dead weight. It seemed an eternity since I had left the comforting shade behind me. How would I ever make it to their table?

"Hey, you guys, I'm here," I shouted, suddenly realizing they had likely not seen me arrive. No one responded. Then they turned as though the sound of my voice had been in limbo. I walked faster. I got to the table, sat down hard, and dropped my pack beside theirs.

"Pat, you've made it! We're a beer ahead," said Wendy. "But don't let that worry you. You won't drink alone."

I joined in their laughter. God, it was good to see them.

"You remember David and Marion, don't you, Pat? We met after mass last night," said Mac.

I shook hands with them. "Glad to see you again." I paused. "Actually it's so good to be here with you." We walked into the cool dark interior of the pub where polished brass gleamed on the countertop and the smell of tapas greeted us.

David was a tall man with the ruddy complexion of a redhead. His girth was sizable. Marion hung back a little. She had a pixie-like face, turned-up nose, and wore plain glasses. Her eyes darted back and forth from David, to me, to Wendy and Mac. Her shyness was painful. I put my arm around her shoulders.

"We've been walking together since early afternoon," David said. "It's been just great. I've always liked you Canucks." He and Mac exchanged a glance. I could sense their ease, their companionship.

My day stretched out behind me: the immense sky spilling out heat, the empty paths, and cool bars where I had stopped on my own.

"How's the day been?" I asked. "Say, did you see those kids in the playground? I stopped and watched them for a few minutes. It was like revisiting our backyard where Dad had built us a swing and teeter-totter. They were doing the same things."

"There was no one there when we went by," said Marion. "I would have loved to see some kids playing around, doing ordinary things."

"Do you remember how great it was when the swing buckled?" Wendy asked. "And then I used to love leaning so far back until I could see the ground and the trees behind me."

"Me, too," I said. "I could nearly touch the top branches of the tree with my feet. My mother used to be so scared, but I knew I wouldn't fall. One of the kids squealed each time the rope buckled. I used to do that, too."

There was a pause. I swirled the beer in my glass, watching the reflections of those scenes in my mind's eye.

"And the teeter-totters! My dad used to bounce me until I started to fall off and was screaming at the top of my lungs. One of the big boys was doing that to his little brother. The little kid was crying for his mother. Nothing changes!"

"My father didn't play with us," Wendy looked at Mac. "Every now and then, when he'd start to play with us, my mother would send him away." There was an awkward silence.

I set my beer glass on the table, which was now covered with tapas dishes and empty glasses. "Now, on to more serious matters. Where are we staying?"

"Funny you should ask," said Mac. He pulled the guidebook out of his pack and opened it to a folded page. "There're a couple of places, small hotels, good prices. Now that you're here, you can ask if they have any rooms."

The sun was beginning to sink and the evening air was cooler when we moved into a small hotel. The corridor leading to our rooms was long and narrow, the linoleum faded and cracked with age. David turned sideways and dropped his huge pack beside the door to let Mac and Wendy pass.

"That looks like quite a weight, David," said Mac. "How are you managing?"

"I'm okay. Really," David replied, his face lined with fatigue. He grabbed the pack and threw it into their room, then turned and grabbed Marion's pack, which was almost as large but bulkier. She turned to him, never taking her eyes off his face.

"Gotta carry a machine for my sinuses or I can't breathe at night. And yeah, you're right, Marion. Don't say it again. I admit that I am tuckered out. It's been a long day."

"Me, too," Wendy's voice floated out from the open door of their room. "I found that ridge climb long and tiring."

The corridor was empty and we had left our doors open. I could hear the quiet in their voices as they set up their rooms and unpacked. My room was cramped. The single bed took up most of the space. The ceiling was high and yellowed with age, with a bald lamp on a cord dangling from the centre of it. I looked in at Wendy and Mac's.

"You've got a palace compared to my closet. Come on over and have a look." They walked a couple of steps and looked through my door.

"This really is minimalist," said Wendy. "Next time let's check out the rooms before we register. You're going to find it stuffy with no windows."

I leaned down to do up my sandals and it all came back. The gross, corpulent man strode by. He made no eye contact. He said nothing. I could smell the body odour. The image evaporated. Had it really happened?

"I almost forgot," I said. "I had an exhibitionist about an hour past the playground." I laughed shortly. "Not much to look at though."

There was shocked silence and then Mac's head appeared around my door. He was chalk white. "Did I hear you correctly? An exhibitionist? He exposed himself to you?"

"Yes," I said.

"And you were alone?"

"Yes. I had walked with others earlier in the day, but I'm usually alone in the afternoon. There was no one around—except him—and me, of course." I laughed again. It sounded thin and hollow in the room.

David stood in their doorway, Marion just behind him. "You're okay? He didn't—do anything?" Marion's voice was squeaky.

"No. No problems. A little scared though." I pulled my clean t-shirt out of my pack. "Well, where's supper tonight?" I asked.

"Someone should have been with you, Pat," said Mac. "You were in danger."

"Well, I have to confess that I couldn't remember the research on those guys. You know, whether they are violent or not. But he wasn't, so I guess I wasn't in danger."

Mac shook his head. "What a terrible experience for you."

"Trust you, Pat, to think of research on the topic," Wendy said with a chuckle, but her eyes were serious.

I looked into their concerned faces and met their eyes. The fear and loathing I had tried to forget after the incident came rushing back. But I was safe now, I reminded myself. I was here with them. They cared about me. I felt my throat tighten. My tears began and I turned away from their concern knowing how close the sobs were.

"I'm okay," I gulped. "Let's go eat. I'm hungry."

The feeling of silk was sleek on my thighs and the bright blue t-shirt felt elegant. My feet in the soft sandals moved easily over the cobblestones.

"I tell you what, Pat. I'll buy the first tapas," said Mac as he put his arm around my shoulders. I smiled up at him. My tears had dried, but my body was still alive with fear and sadness. I had felt so alone and vulnerable after the incident. And still did.

As we passed a small noisy bar, rich fragrant aromas surrounded us. "Let's stop here," said Marion. "It smells good."

The bar was full of people. They glanced at us without missing a beat in their conversations. Behind the bar stood two men dressed in white shirts, their black hair slicked back. The one was pouring drinks as they were called out to him; the other was serving steaming tapas. We stood transfixed by the sight of shrimp, sliced hams, olives.

"Do you know, I think I missed lunch today," I said.

"How's about some tiger shrimp?" asked Mac as he pointed to the pan. The barman slid a dish of it across the counter in front of Wendy before anyone could speak.

"What a feast," said Wendy biting her first shrimp in half. "My God, these are wonderful."

I looked at my friends, beer in hand, eyes overly bright. We're all a bit high, I thought. We had burned up a lot of energy and hadn't eaten enough during the day. The beer had gone straight to our heads.

Marion pointed to a pan containing slices of something bathed in a red sauce. "That looks yummy," she said in her Aussie accent. "What are they?"

I leaned over the counter and asked, "¿Qué es eso?"

The dark eyes fixed on mine. "These are pigs' ears, señora," he replied, putting the ladle into the rich sauce. "How much would you like?"

"We'll try a small serving." I translated for Wendy. Mac looked slightly ill. The barman reached over and a square clay bowl arrived before us. The smell was distinctive and not very pleasant. I ordered more beer.

"Okay, who's first?" asked Mac.

Marion picked up a small toothpick and jabbed at an ear. It slid out of her grasp. She plunged the pick in again, this time with success. What appeared before her was the tip of an ear. The sauce was clinging to it, mostly along what looked to be hair or bristles. My stomach clenched in anticipation as I speared another slice of an ear. Once in my mouth, the flavour of the sauce overpowered the taste of the ear. But nothing could disguise its rubbery texture and soft, marinated bristles. I chewed rapidly and compulsively. With a gulp it descended.

"Have another one, Pat," David encouraged me. "They're really good, eh?"

I looked at his clean plate and fixed him in a direct stare. "So tell me, how would you know?"

"Marion, how many have you eaten?" asked Wendy.

"Same number as you, of course," she replied, her lips pursed, sauce on her chin.

"But I've only had two. I think you've passed me."

"Come on, Marion," said David. "We've been counting—and I'll bet you won't leave that last one either." He folded his arms and stared at her. As if to prove his point she scooped the last slice of ear out of the sauce, took a slice of bread, and wiped out the bowl. Her face was screwed slightly as she chewed hard. Her eyes were cold.

"What difference does it make to you?" she demanded. "You won't even stoop to trying them. If you had ever been hungry, really hungry, you'd know that a person would try anything without turning up his nose like you do."

He looked at her for a long time, not smiling, inscrutable. Marion put the toothpick on the edge of the pan. "Shall we go find a restaurant?" she asked.

We paid and moved through the crowd, which was growing bigger and noisier.

"I don't think we need anything more to eat," said David. "That's about done it, I reckon. It sure cost enough."

What kind of a guy was this? He apparently had no sympathy for his wife and was now offering a decision on dinner without asking for other opinions. Not my idea of a travelling companion.

"Not for me—I want a meal—meat and veggies and red wine," I announced.

"Me, too," said Mac.

Wendy looked around and then pointed to the far corner. "I can see a restaurant sign on the other side of this plaza. Let's give it a try."

It was velvety black when we finally left the restaurant. As we walked beneath the arcades and past the faint light of lampposts, the familiar feeling of sadness returned. It invaded my body and left me without words. A silence had fallen on the group. Our footsteps echoed slightly across the empty plaza.

"When do you want to leave tomorrow?" asked David. I waited for the answer. Wendy, Mac, and I had had this conversation again last night. "Remember how hot it was today? Well, I saw a weather map on the television. It looks to be another hot one—well over thirty degrees. I think we should be on the Camino no later than seven," he announced.

"I agree." The sound of Wendy's voice was hushed as we passed under another arcade.

"David's right. It gave us a couple of hours of cooler walking today," said Marion.

"And we, on the other hand, really slogged it out," Wendy's voice was pointed.

I could feel my resistance building again. Why was I so stubborn about this? Why not just agree? Leaving early had advantages. I listened to the discussion between the two couples. Mac was maintaining his stand that eight o'clock was still cool enough and plenty early. I opened my mouth to agree but changed my mind.

"So we agree to leave by seven?" David sounded firm.

Mac paused audibly, then said, "I guess I have to agree. If it's hotter again tomorrow, an early start …" He looked in my direction. I nodded but said nothing.

I walked on in silence. It occurred to me that I had nothing to say against the decision, not really. I didn't disagree. And in an awkward way I really had nothing to say in support of it, either. I was in a void somewhere out of contact.

In any case, departure wasn't the issue. Would departure time have made any difference this afternoon? The real problem was that no one had been with me. I had faced it alone. What were the chances I'd walk alone tomorrow? Barring something extraordinary, it would be a day like the others. Anything could happen. That's the issue, I thought: the issue I refused to talk about before dinner back at the hotel.

I recalled our morning. The three of us had chatted over coffee before Wendy and Mac headed off. Their conversation was couples' talk, like a dance. They touched unconsciously, with the obvious intimacy and ease of daily habits, of knowing each other. For me, that sense of everyday, taken-for-granted intimacy was missing. I was the outsider.

CHAPTER 5

THE ENERGY
OF THE EARTH

I pulled the sock up gingerly, trying not to break the blister. I stood up and took several steps; the boot felt tight and uncomfortable. I sat down and began to work on my other foot. It'll be like yesterday, I thought. Sensitive to begin with, then no problem. There was a soft knock at the door. "¿Sí?" I said hesitantly.

"Pat, we're heading down for coffee. You ready?" It was Mac's voice.

"I'll be right down. Just need a couple of minutes," I replied. I applied some antibiotic cream, cut off another piece of bandage, and tied up the boot. Then, anxious to catch up, I stepped quickly into the hall. Misery and worn-out hope seemed embedded in the faded wallpaper and the muted odours of the convent where nuns had lived for centuries.

The snap of the *minutier* triggered the hall light and I saw three people approaching. Although they were talking softly I could hear the French cadence.

"Bonjour," I said. "Je m'appelle Pat."

The man gestured to the two women. "Ma femme, Nicole, et notre amie, Sylvie. Et moi, André. We're Swiss." The light caught their silver-grey hair as we shook hands. How attractive they are, I thought. We started down the stairs, walking in friendly rhythm.

"My friends are over there," I said, pointing to the table where the two couples sat. "Likely see you later."

I trudged over to the table, pack on one shoulder. Marion's glasses were fogged from the steam of her coffee. David had attached corks to the rim of his hat to discourage the flies he'd been complaining about. The corks bobbled as he lowered his head to drink. The sound of slurping grated on my nerves. No one said a word. I put the pack on a chair and started for the counter.

"I'll get you a coffee, Pat," Mac said. "Just sit down and have one of those brioches." He was back almost immediately. I felt a surge of gratitude. I buttered the brioche, added some marmalade from my pack, and dunked it. As I twisted my head to eat, the coffee dribbled down my chin.

"Well," said Wendy, "it's time to hit the road—or should I call it the *senda* like the Spanish do?" They stood up as one and put on their packs. I stuffed the last of the brioche into my mouth and swung the pack on my back. It settled there like an old familiar friend. I turned just as Marion opened the door onto the darkened plaza. The cold air hit my bare legs and I faced the blackness of the morning. I sensed the golden warmth of the coffee shop behind me. I could almost hear the sleepy voices; see the slow movements, another world. I asked myself why I had followed the group plan and why I was now rushing to join them. The clock on the church tower hadn't even rung seven o'clock. A solitary street lamp cast a soft light on the stones of the town wall as we headed out across the plaza in search of the mystical yellow arrow.

"It's over here," Wendy whispered. "Come on! It's right here." I squinted into the darkness. I could just make her out against the light brown of the stones. We abandoned our search and followed her. The road was narrow. It wended left, then right, and soon we were on the outskirts of Pamplona. A grey, ghostly signpost and a yellow arrow marked the path to Puente la Reina.

I reached out and touched the letters. That was when it began. At first I felt a tingling sensation in my thighs. Then the pulsations moved up and down my legs. I looked ahead anxiously. Wendy and Mac were slightly ahead of me engrossed in conversation.

I called out to them. "Hey, can you feel this strange …?" They walked on, oblivious. The energy surged into my core and I stood stock still, my head spinning. A couple of hikers walked by calling out "Buen Camino" as they passed. They looked at me curiously as though about to speak but hurried on. The surges became stronger, slowed, then stopped.

So this must be what some writers described as the "ley lines." The earth's crust was purportedly thinnest under the Camino, which meant that the vibrations—the very energy of the earth—could be felt here according to these new age thinkers. I had been so skeptical when I read about this back in Calgary. Now, standing here in Spain, my pack on my back, my skepticism dissolved; I was struck dumb.

In that fleeting moment I saw again the thousands who had passed by here. I wondered how many had felt these surges. Like us, they were vulnerable. They had made a commitment. What a mysterious feat, this pilgrimage. How compelling its markers. We had not questioned it since we set foot on it that first morning. We had followed it along freeways, up ancient paths, and over Roman bridges. Our destination was Santiago. There was no turning back.

The sunrise was magical. The light touched the highest peaks first; the shadows deepened in the forest and in the valley ahead of us. Like a blush, the colour filled the sky and penetrated the depths of the dark wells around the trees, touching the trunks with orange. As day broke, pilgrims no longer whispered but spoke, and from time to time there was laughter. The senda was crowded that morning as though everyone was going to the local market.

I started up a steep path and looked back several times at the panorama of Pamplona bathed in the sunlight. As I neared Alto de Perdón, the climb grew even steeper and the path narrow and rocky. I heard a low eerie noise. Startled, I looked around, saw Wendy, and heard her laughter.

"It's not alive, Pat," she shouted. "It's the wind in those windmills! Doesn't it remind you of home?"

"Yes," I shouted, my voice swept away by the strong wind. I hurried to catch up to them. We followed the ridge and saw the line of bold, two-dimensional figures cut out of cast iron. Exposure to the wind, rain, and snow had rusted them. They were our height and shape and, I thought, like us they were caught in time. Some strained against the wind, their staves planted in front of them; others were holding onto their hats. A small, forlorn donkey, burdened down by a pack, stood beside two people.

"I feel a kinship with him," I said, pointing to the donkey. "Just look how we are both hunched over by the weight of our burdens." I scrunched my shoulders and bent over, one hand holding onto my pack.

"I'll capture that for you—and posterity," David said, getting his camera. "Choose a pilgrim to walk with." We spread out among the statues choosing the one we wanted to stand beside. Then we set off together. I dropped back behind David and Marion. Wendy and Mac stepped into the lead. The last glimpse I had of them, they were walking side by side, filling the path as it turned sharply upward. Then they were gone. The sun lit the dewdrops on a spider's web, which hung not far from the trail. They sparkled and shimmered. The web had torn slightly but was still attached to the branches. As I walked I concentrated on the shadows of the Camino.

In *The Pilgrimage*, Coelho had suggested several different meditations. This morning I was drawn to his suggestion of starting with the shadows of the day. The rhythm of my pace lulled me, and my mind became tranquil. My boots were slightly scuffed and dusty and the knob of the walking stick balanced easily in my hand. The sense of meditation grew slowly, gaining its own reality. The shadow of my silhouette was the first focus. I could see the movement, the outline of my body. My legs were shortened by the angle of the sun and my upper body and head were elongated. Turning my head didn't change the shadow. What's really there, I wondered. There's only a distorted outline, nothing of reality—or was there? I focused on the proportions. The lack of detail, of colour and emotions stood out. I watched as the shortened legs carried me along at my slow pace. I thought with amusement, it's clearly because my legs are too short! Nearby in some bushes, a bird began to sing. I felt its warble.

As I approached a tilled field, the thistles lining the ditch stood out against the cobalt sky, throwing shadows on the senda. Intrigued, I looked closely at several and then stopped to study them. The shadows of the stems were often obvious and I could identify the shapes of the thistles themselves. I stared at the shadows. Some were mere splotches, impossible to identify and to relate to other parts of the plants. Still others, main branches, stood out clearly. Yet, in one shadow, I could see a branch that stood alone, not connected to anything. With some of the shadows, I imagined connections and filled in what I thought was the silhouette of the plant. It reminded me of the complex interrelated experiences of relationships, of living, and of the Camino. I looked up to study the plants themselves and realized with a shock that the shadows, for the most part, did not represent the physical reality of the plants. They were ghostly evocations but not representations. Many of the connections I had made were in my head, not part of what I was observing. They were based on my ideas about plants rather than the shadows.

Suddenly feeling foolish standing alone like this, I started walking, found my pace, and swung my stick rhythmically. Confusion overwhelmed me. So what is reality? Like Plato in the cave I wondered about what I had seen. The shadows cast in comparison with the reality of the heat and the plants occupied my thinking. What are these different realities? How true that many experiences, like the shadows, seem disconnected and yet in one reality they are an integral part of the whole, linked simply and coherently to make up the whole. It is in our interpretations that they take on another meaning.

It was near lunch when I heard people speaking French and picked up my pace in anticipation of company. As I rounded the steep rocky turn, I saw the Swiss I had met in the hotel this morning. They were sitting on a blanket spread out beneath some pines. André had a glass of wine in his hand. He was stretched out, leaning back, his hand on Nicole's ankle. Sylvie sat to one side bringing out the cold cuts and bread from her pack. "Come over here, Patricia!" André called out. "Come stay a while with us. You'll enjoy this wine and we'd love your company."

I stopped and dropped my pack. "Do you remember *The Seventh Seal*? The Bergman movie?"

"Mais, oui," said Sylvie. "Who doesn't remember it? It was a masterpiece. I think you are talking about the scene when the knight stops with the family in that little meadow, non? They have some wine and strawberries together."

"Yes, that's it," I replied. "And they begged him to stay, but he continued his quest. Just like me. I, too, will keep on moving."

"Oh, don't do that." André's voice was seductive. "You must stop here, with us. You are walking alone. It must be lonely. Why don't your friends wait for you? Is this a Canadian habit?"

They looked at me expectantly. I sensed their compassion and their curiosity.

"Well, as you know I am a slow walker …"

"Mais, non, Patricia! You do just fine," André insisted. He held out the bottle of wine. "Have a glass."

"Nope, thanks, but I'm going to keep moving. They're faster than I am. We get together at the end of the day. It's not a problem."

André shrugged his shoulders and recapped the wine.

"Well, then we'll see you this evening?" asked Sylvie.

"You can count on it," I said as I swung the pack on my back and started down the path stepping carefully over rocks. I was soon out of hearing. I longed to go back, to sit and chat. I thought of returning but kept on walking. The sun was hot and insistent and my shadow was nonexistent.

It was afternoon when I finally caught up with my group sitting at a long wooden table in a small plaza. The owner came out and took my order.

Squinting against the bright sunlight, I announced, "I've had a great time meditating on shadows."

Mac sipped his beer and said, "Is that why you're not keeping up?" They all looked at Mac and then at me. The laughter was forced.

"No, seriously," I insisted. "Look at the shadows while you're walking and see what that teaches you. Who knows, Wendy, it might even be a metaphor!"

She smiled and took a sip of her wine. David and Marion looked at me, then at each other.

"Upward and onward," David suggested as he stood up and swung on his pack.

"Are you stopping in Eunate to see the church?" I asked. "It is apparently the most beautiful of the Camino."

"We haven't really talked about it," said Wendy. "But we'll likely see you there."

I stopped near the turnoff for Eunate and sat down for coffee. A tall waitress came out and asked for my order. "Un café con leche y una … biscota?" I gestured to the plate of croissants. She nodded and put one on a brilliant blue plate. I sat down at an empty table just as the steaming coffee arrived. I dunked the croissant and tapped it against the cup. I watched other tables fill with pilgrims and listened to the staccato of Spanish mingled with other languages. I rolled my head back and gazed with intense pleasure at the brilliant blue sky. My body relaxed on the wooden chair and I stretched out my legs. I took the guidebook out of my pack. Eunate was only four kilometres off the path. I was reading about the church when a man's voice interrupted my reading. "Would you mind if we sat at your table?"

"Please." I gestured to the chairs and extended my hand. "I'm from Western Canada. My name's Pat."

"My name is Will and this is my son Erik." He put his hand on the young man's shoulder. "We are from Holland and visiting the churches of the Camino." The men were tall, slim, and blond. I could see they were related.

"I see you are reading the guidebook. Are you checking out Eunate?" Erik asked.

"It sounds exceptionally beautiful so, yes, I thought I'd take the detour. How about you?"

"It is one of our main reasons for doing this part of the Camino. We have spent our time studying churches—although they are all Catholic. We are Protestants. What I love is styles of architecture and Erik is taken with paintings, interiors, sculptures, and design."

"I can relate to that," I replied. "I love the beauty of the stained glass and how it helped people to understand." I paused and added lamely, "Of course, Luther had something to say about that." The three of us laughed.

"The important thing is that you know what it is to be passionate about something," Will stated, looking me in the eye and smiling. "So, how about Eunate?" He took out a Dutch guide and translated. "This church is octagonal, which is the style of the Church of the Holy Sepulchre in Jerusalem, but no one knows its origins for certain. Graves containing scallop shells have been discovered between the church and the outside walls."

I had leaned forward and was listening intently when he stopped reading and said, "Well, shall we walk together?"

It was hard to say "no" to them. Will's eyes were light piercing blue. I felt as though he were reading my thoughts as I hesitated. I was confident I'd enjoy their company, but I didn't want to be forced into conversation. And I realized I was enjoying meditating as I walked alone.

"Yes, Will," I said in spite of myself. "I'd love to join you." I swung my pack and felt it settle on my back with such familiarity. I tugged at the bellyband and secured it against my body. They moved quickly along the pebbled path. For a moment I was painfully aware of my short, round legs, old leather boots, and sweat-stained shorts. A white line of salt edged my belt. I had washed my t-shirt the night before, but it was showing signs of wear. The shoulders were beaded from the straps of my pack. The red shirt, which I started off the mornings with, was crumpled and shoved between the straps on the back of the pack. The silence became companionable. We covered the distance with the ease that comes from knowing how to walk your pace.

Eunate was small and soft grey in the intense heat of the day. A short stone wall wound around it, protecting it from close contact with street traffic. We had to step down to enter the main door. The large iron padlock was closed.

"I'll find us a key," said Erik, heading for a nearby bar, which was full of people. He returned minutes later with a large, ancient key in his hand.

"They've had trouble with vandalism lately," he said as he cranked the key to the left. It opened and we walked into splendour.

The church was small but of perfect proportions. Its walls rose straight and fluid in the light. Circling the cupola were stained glass windows. These were not the rose windows of the gothic cathedrals, but rather plain filters for the midday sun. The walls were dappled with their soft yellow and vague rose reflections. The church was empty except for us—and the man on the cross. He was so thin, so fragile and yet dominated the space. His skin was waxen and pale. I stepped closer; my eyes blurred. There was passivity in the line of his body that spoke of resignation, of acceptance, of forgiveness. His eyes were closed and I could just make out the eyelashes that touched his cheeks. His presence seemed ephemeral, barely physical. Although nailed to the cross, his body hung lightly as though without heft. His arms didn't bend with his weight; his feet crossed modestly. There he was, now a grown man, pinioned for his beliefs against the mathematics of the cross. I sat down in the centre of the church; I couldn't take my eyes off him. Where was she? Had she watched? What had been her path since she gave birth? How had she lived through the events of his life with her overwhelming love?

The door creaked open and a woman came in. "Ah," I heard her breathe out. She came closer to where I was and sat cross-legged on the floor. I took my eyes off him and looked at her. We made eye contact; she touched my arm and then turned back to him. Not a word was said. The image of a statue, a pieta, in another cathedral came to mind unbidden. Mary was sitting, head tilted to one side, looking down on the body of her son. Her left hand cradled his head, which had lolled to one side. One of his arms hung down, a dead weight. His body crossed hers, feet touching the ground. How did she manage to hold him, to keep him from falling, I wondered. Her face was without expression as though numbed by the reality of her son's lifeless body against hers.

I sensed more people coming into the silence and I looked up to see Will and his son nod to me as they left the church. I was transfixed, unable and unwilling to leave.

I thought back to churches, large, small, and ancient, that I had visited over the years. The smell of incense and tired bodies had accumulated over the centuries and permeated all the buildings. And yet this poignant, simple story in all its beauty spoke to everyone in spite of declining attendance and shortages of priests and nuns.

. . .

I heard the sound of their voices and laughter as I entered the plaza in Puente de la Reina. They were sitting at a small bar. Wendy and Marion were on a bench, the two men in front of them. Someone's comment had provoked the laughter. They were all looking at Mac. He had his hands on his knees, head back, laughing.

Marion called out, "Come on over here! We've waited for you—but not for the beer."

My pack dropped with a thud on the cobblestones. "Order another beer, David," I said, smiling.

Marion was in charge. "Then we'll have to find a place to eat. There are some really good restaurants here according to my guidebook."

The beer slid down my throat easing the parched feeling.

"So, how was your day?" I asked.

David answered. "Well, we kept up with these two greyhounds here." He looked at Mac with great admiration. "I didn't know that Canadians could move so fast."

"Our politics aren't fast, David, but the footwork is. We're generally fleeing some conflict or Calgary winters as the case may be," Mac explained. We all laughed.

My shoulders relaxed. The chair felt so good, so easy. God, it had been a long, hard day, I thought, emotionally and physically. I bent over and undid my boots then eased my feet out and wiggled my toes. The blood circulated into them and the pain was sharp.

"How was your day, Pat?" asked Wendy tentatively.

"Like the landscape, up and down. But I got here, Wendy. And that's what counts."

"How are your blisters?" Mac had a tense and worried look. He was squinting slightly in the sun. I could feel the empathy in the group.

"I just don't pay attention to them," I lied. "My feet do the job—and do it better when there's good conversation. But right now I think I'll put Andrea's plan in place." I started to get up from the table.

"And what is that?" Marion queried.

"Well, my friend Andrea says you need a ritual to mark the end of walking. Take a shower, change into evening gear, find a book, and go to a nice bar—work's done, enjoy being in Spain. So, for me, I think maybe a shower and a change of clothes would make this day perfect."

There was a pause as they stared at me. I smiled back at them. "Then we can find something to eat and olé! A good evening for all."

My room was painted white with high ceilings and French doors. It was cool and silent. I stretched out on the bed with a sense of gratitude. We've only done ninety kilometres—a little more than a tenth of the Camino. I felt the rough texture of the sheets. Before this my longest walk had been the GR20 across Corsica. It was 180 kilometres and had taken ten days. I remembered the heat, the sweat, and the fragrance of rosemary as we scrambled up rock faces. I was the slowest then, too. But this Camino was demanding in a way I couldn't put my finger on. In Corsica I had become bored with walking and dropped out for a day while the group went climbing. I had read a book. It had been such a relief to do something other than walk. Who knows? At some point the Camino might have the same effect. I might get bored. I could always take a bus, stay in a city for a couple of days. Maybe Burgos. I wanted to spend time at the cathedral there anyway. I could let them catch up. Not soon, of course, but it was an option. I rose with a sigh and grabbed a towel. The shower was hot and pounded down on my back.

We began our search for a restaurant, one that catered to pilgrims, and noticed people walking toward a sign with a crossed knife and fork. The dining room was small, full of pilgrims and the sounds of other languages. There was a television at the bar and we could hear the olés at a bullfight.

Marion flinched. "I hate violence toward animals," she said as she hurried past the bar.

"Have you ever seen a bullfight, Marion?" I asked, walking behind her as we headed toward the tables.

"No, and I'll never go to one," she shuddered, eyes fixed on a table at the back of the restaurant.

"Believe me," I said, "at the first bullfight I saw what struck me was that the bull was no victim. He was a massive animal. He charged into the ring and challenged everyone. They all took cover behind the protective walls and peered over them anxiously. I saw one toreador chewing on his cape! Death was there that afternoon, but there was no guarantee who would be chosen." There was a roar from the TV set and several of the patrons cheered.

"That's easy to say, Pat," David commented. "But there aren't nearly as many dead matadors as there are bulls."

"All, or at least many, of the great matadors have died in the ring," I pointed out. "It's just not a sure thing, killing the bull."

Marion was still scanning the room for a place to sit.

"Look, there's Geoff," Wendy pointed out the American we had met earlier. "And isn't that Franz and Helmut?" She waved and called out, "Buen Camino, amigos." They looked up at the sound of her voice and beckoned us over. Geoff scurried around to find an extra chair. When the waiter arrived we ordered several carafes of wine.

It was dark when we left. The sky was a curious lime colour along the horizon and the dome was deep blue. I breathed deeply, enjoying the air and the smells of cooking. David and Marion walked slowly. He had his arm around her shoulders. She looked small and fragile beside him.

"Let's stop for a cognac," Mac suggested.

"No, mate, I think we'll just head back," David replied. They hugged us and headed down a narrow street leading to the hostel.

We walked on, savouring the evening. "I think that money's a constant problem for them," said Mac empathetically. "That's why they're staying in refugios."

"You could call them albergues," Wendy said. "It sounds so much more—I don't know—romantic?"

"There's no romance in those double-layered bunk beds with twenty other people snoring beside you," Mac laughed. "It's a long ways from romantic!"

Our cognacs came in large snifters, which were half full. "Next time we'll share one between us," Wendy commented. I looked at my friends. It was still our Camino no matter who joined us, I thought.

We walked quietly to the small convent where we had booked rooms. Mac reached up and rang the bell. The buzzer answered shrilly and we heard the ancient locks slide open. It was dark in the corridor. I pushed the minutier, the lights came on, and we walked up the short flight of stairs. A nun stood at the top of the steps, silhouetted in the feeble light. Her black habit touched the floor and the white wimple stood out sharply. She greeted us with a smile and handed us our keys. The minutier turned off and I whispered, "Buenas noches" as we headed to our rooms.

"See you just before six-thirty, Pat," Wendy reminded me.

The room was small with a narrow, single bed. A candle stood on the night table beside a Bible. The bathroom was tiny, but as I washed my face in the cold water I was grateful for the privacy. The bed squeaked as I stretched out on it. The blankets were thin and worn, a reminder that the convent was on a strict budget. I wondered how long they had been renting out rooms. I felt my eyes get heavier. I heard vaguely the sounds of other pilgrims coming in, doors shutting. Then nothing, as sleep came.

• • •

The sound of heavy boots filled me with terror. They stopped beside my bed. The odour of a dirty body filled my nostrils. Pale grey eyes locked on mine. I could see the distorted pores on his nose. He gestured to his penis, grinning.

With a gasp I found myself sitting upright, my heart pounding. I stared into the darkness. Was he really here? I had seen him. He was here. He was with me. I scanned the walls. No, there was no one in the room. I sank back into bed, sweat on my palms and under my arms. I tossed and turned, afraid to trust the sleep that I needed so desperately.

—∞∞∞—

CHAPTER 6

A PRAYER

The small clock on the night table showed it was six-fifteen. I looked around the room, begging that it had been a bad dream. The interior was stark and silent. The sink and furniture were a testimony to reality. Through the lace curtains on the window I could see the dark street and its cobblestones. A trickle of sunlight settled on the floor near the windows reminding me that the day was beginning and would bring its gifts and sorrows.

I walked into the small shop to the welcome fragrance of coffee. Wendy had rummaged in her backpack and was sharing cheese and some bread from yesterday.

"Have some bread, Pat," she offered. "They are all out of food this morning."

"Well," said David, "Marion and I talked last night and we have decided to stay here for a couple of days to get things organized. We want to send some of the stuff from our packs back to Australia, get our tickets changed. You know the kind of stuff."

"David, I admire you for that decision," I said. "Those packs of yours are a real challenge. They must weigh a ton."

"You're too right," Marion chimed in. "I wanted to do this earlier, but

David is so enjoying walking with you. So last night we decided to stay here and agree on where to meet up with you later. We can do this because of your scope and sequence, Mac," she added. Mac smiled modestly and we all laughed.

"Give us anything you want shipped back to Canada. We'll have enough time to find boxes and paper. We'd be glad to help. That's if you want to get rid of some weight," Marion urged.

I dunked the heel of bread in the hot coffee. "I know this isn't an early morning topic, but we haven't slept in a refugio yet." I looked at Wendy and Mac. "So maybe I could just send back my sleeping bag? It's a good three kilos of weight I could do without."

"Good opportunity," said Mac. "I'm all for that."

Wendy scowled at him. "You're limiting our options, Mac," she reminded him.

He grinned boyishly. "Just keeping other advantages open," he said, and gave her a hug.

"You know, we could just stop here ourselves," I suggested. I looked up from my coffee at my friends, their faces wreathed with early morning smiles.

"Why on earth would we do that?" Mac queried.

"Well, we've known each other for a long time. But in some ways we don't know each other at all. It's been years since we first met. We could just hang out here, walk around, and enjoy the town. Tell each other stories. Wander off tomorrow—well, we could even spend a couple of days. We have the time."

Their smiles had disappeared and I could feel the conviction in my voice growing thin. There was a silence.

"I thought about this last night when we got back. You know, we aren't getting much talk time. We each walk at our own pace during the day," I added.

Surprise registered on their faces. "But we'll get to know each other better over the length of the Camino. After all, we are together in the morning and again all evening," Wendy said. "Why take time out? We aren't going that fast as it is."

I shrugged. "Yeah, I guess there are lots of ways to get to know each other. And we've got likely thirty days before we get to Santiago," I agreed.

David and Marion laughed. "This must be the Canadian style of negotiating," David quipped. "You'd all agreed before I got the gist of the problem."

We hugged them and promised to meet in Logroño in three days.

The sun was high when we found the Camino signpost. I watched Wendy and Mac move ahead at their quick pace. There was a sense of languor within me, of timelessness. As the sky began to lighten, I reminded myself that each day was to be cherished. The experience of the walk unfolded moment by moment. I had only to be aware of it.

Several hours later I entered Mañeru and began to stroll its tree-lined streets. It was beautiful just as the guidebook described it. Before long, I noticed a sign to visit the Iglesia de San Pedro, a neoclassical church set back off the avenue among grand houses. A sudden desire to be inside—to see the altar and the Stations of the Cross—overwhelmed me. I wanted to feel the peace I often experienced in Catholic churches. The door was open. As my eyes adjusted to the darkness, I could make out several groups of adults and children. It must be a saint's day, I thought. The smell of incense, the soft light of candles burning on the altar, and the sight of kneeling bodies swept over me. I stopped and knelt at the pew. As I sat down, a hand tapped my shoulder. I turned and made out the features of a man dressed in a cassock.

"¿Sí?" I asked. He replied in rapid Spanish, gesturing toward the plaque at the end of the pew. Seeing that I didn't understand, he shook his head and pointed to another pew. I smiled, nodded, and sat down just as the music of the morning service began and the priest called his parishioners to mass.

As he began I was aware of movement behind me. Looking over my shoulder I saw a woman, limping badly, heading toward a pew. Her progress down the aisle was slow and painful. She paused, caught her breath, and moved with difficulty to a pew where there was room. As she got there, the family turned to look at her. The father scowled. Beside him, her face partly eclipsed from my view, sat his wife in a dark suit. The three children beside her also turned to look at the crippled woman. She laboured to sit down beside them. The man's body stiffened. He shook his head at her. His wife leaned forward and hissed something to her husband. Startled, the woman turned to face them. He said something and pointed to the end of the pew. She bowed her head, made a gesture to her leg brace. He shook his head again, pointing to the back of the church. Leaning heavily on her cane, the woman rose and made her way back. I sat in stunned silence. The family turned their attention back to the priest.

Once again in the heat of the sun in front of the church, I looked for the flechas, indicating the Camino. As I searched, an elderly woman came up and asked me if I was searching for the Camino.

"Sí," I replied.

"Come with me." She laid a hand on my arm and smiled up at me. "It's over this way. I will show you. As a young woman I did all of the Camino. Are you walking all of it?"

Numbed by her kindness, I felt my throat tighten and the tears well up. I rubbed my eyes and said, "Sí, the whole Camino." She stopped at the lights, pointing to the sign and the path. Then, she took my face in her hands. Looking deeply into my eyes, she said, "Buen Camino—you will find what you search for." And she was gone.

I started up the path, taken aback by my reaction to her compassion and insight. I looked up at the pink sky, allowing myself to dwell in the emotions welling up in me. I knew how vulnerable I was. I was stripped of the defences I took for granted back home. In some way I was naked, as though reborn. As the familiar anxiety ran through me I remembered that anxiety is a way of knowing. What is it that I know, I puzzled.

I picked up my pace slightly. The path twisted and turned among the large boulders. Here and there, gnarled ancient trees eked out an existence in the rocky soil. I stopped to touch one of them and discovered that the leaves were prickly and stiff.

Slowly but surely I walked up the ridge. My feet were hurting immensely. In the last two days, after about five hours of walking, the pain would begin. Then I took painkillers, although the pain seemed beyond control. I was on my own, trudging along slowly when I arrived at the top of the ridge. The barren landscape stretched in all directions. There was no greenery, no farmed land. A large metal cross stood immutable against the sharp sky. The scraggly trees ranged back from it as though in awe. Under the cross there were folded pieces of white paper barely visible beneath the large stones placed on them. Someone had tied a ribbon to the cross, and it lifted and floated with the random breezes from the valley. I sat on the wooden bench. Sharp penetrating pain filled my feet as the blood flow changed.

"Jesus," I exclaimed. "Jesus." I let my head roll back and rubbed my eyes. It'll soon stop, I thought, bound to. Nothing this bad can go on. Slowly, the pain abated. I looked around guardedly. There was no one approaching. I searched quickly in my pack and found a piece of paper and a pen. What will I write, I wondered. What's appropriate for an agnostic to pray for—and to whom do I address this? Never mind the details, I thought, just get it over with before someone sees you. The words flowed without effort. "I pray for divine intervention so that my feet won't hurt so much."

I hesitated. Should I sign it? I re-read the message in my handwriting. It was on the back of an old bank form. Then I saw two pilgrims approaching. I quickly found a rock and placed my prayer with the hundreds of others at the foot of the cross. I was sitting on the bench when the two women arrived. Hearing the cadence of their voices I knew they were French. My heart quickened at the thought of some company.

I stood up, like a welcoming committee, I thought. Moments later, two dark-haired women appeared, looking at each other and laughing. Their laughter was strong, vibrant, the laughter of good friends.

"Bonjour," I said and, unable to resist, I joined in the laughter. They came over to the bench and sat down.

"Whew! It's a long way up, n'est-ce pas?" said one. "I am Jeanne. We are from Toulon. Do you know it? On the Mediterranean coast?" I nodded.

"And my friend, Katrina, Katie."

I introduced myself and we sat staring at the scene before us. The wind had picked up and the clouds were skittering across the sky.

"Why are you walking the Camino de Santiago?" Katie's voice broke the silence with a flourish.

"At this moment, I'm not too sure. My feet are killing me," I replied in French. "But to answer your question, the common reasons. You know, to see the country, the churches, practise my Spanish. How about you?"

"My time on the Camino," replied Jeanne "is to pray for the soul of my sister who died of cancer last year. She was my older sister. Only forty-three years old. Katie is my closest friend and this is now the second year she comes with me to walk for two weeks."

"Oui," said Katie, "our husbands are in Toulon. They stay there, look after the kids, and earn money so we can walk." Their laughter was conspiratorial.

"How far will you walk today?" I asked.

"We'll stop when we've finished," said Jeanne. She was small, vivacious, and dark.

Aha, I thought. I am right. The French don't do scope and sequence. We sat together on the bench chatting in French.

I found myself staring at my boots. The pain was still there. "My feet are killing me," I confided again.

They both grinned at me. "Ours, too."

I felt the empathy between us. Before I could stop myself, I said, "Would you mind if I walk with you for an hour? I am not a fast walker, but I really need some company. Of course, if you don't want to …"

"Don't be silly," interrupted Jeanne. "We'll walk together to Los Arcos."

"That's wonderful," I said, my eyes floating behind my dark glasses. "That's where I am meeting the other Canadians I'm with."

The pain settled in my feet and moved up to my knees as we began going down the rocky slope together. A couple of hours later, we stopped and stretched out in the shade of a church door, stocking feet up against the stone wall. I was lying in a dream-like state, thinking about nothing, revelling in the warmth of being with kindred souls. This is probably what it has always been like, I thought to myself. Pilgrims meeting pilgrims, random acts of kindness. How ageless! I turned my head to look at the plaza. The heat was shimmering. There was no one to be seen.

Katie's voice broke into my thoughts. "Eh, bien, les amies, on y va?" We laced up our boots, picked up our packs, and walked across the plaza. The sun was losing some of its heat. The late afternoon sky looked mellow. We were rested and we were heading for Los Arcos.

Three hours later, laughing and talking, we walked into the outskirts of the town. A little further along, I saw Mac and Wendy coming along the path.

"We were so worried," said Wendy. "Are you okay?"

"Okay? Je viens de passer ..." I stopped and looked at them. "Just look what happens to me when I speak French all day. This has been my best day on the Camino," I said, grinning. I hugged Jeanne and Katie, who were staying in an albergue. "You don't know it, but you are the first answer I've ever had to a prayer!"

Jeanne looked quietly into my eyes. "We always meet someone when we need someone," she said. "Trust me, I know."

I turned to Wendy and Mac and gave them a big hug.

"Okay, you guys! It's so good to see you. Let's have a beer!" We set off with great purpose, our arms linked.

Not long after, showered and clean, we headed off to eat in a well-known restaurant specializing in local produce. We were standing at the corner of a cobblestone street searching our town map when a Spaniard stopped and asked us what we were looking for. He was a short, middle-aged man with black, sparkling eyes. Like others of this area, his face was tanned, deeply creased, and weathered.

I explained our search for the restaurant. He pulled me close to him. I could smell the garlic and stale wine on his breath.

"Señora," he whispered in my ear, "I know a much better restaurant at a much better price."

"So what's up, Pat?" asked Wendy.

"Well, it's like this. This gentleman knows of an excellent local restaurant at a better price and he'd like to show us there. What do you think? I mean it won't be gourmet, but he assures me it is good."

I looked at him again skeptically. He was impeccably groomed in clothes of another era. His brown shoes shone and his pants were pressed, the crease perfect. But did that make him an expert on restaurants?

I shrugged. "Look, why not? We know lots of gourmet restaurants. This will be an experience." I nodded to him. "Let's go."

He smiled and began to tell me the history of the restaurant, his home, and his life now that his wife had died. I listened to the humble story of this proud man. His children had moved into the city. He stayed here to be with his friends, although his daughters often asked him to move.

"De aquí soy," he said. "I'm from *here*."

Later, seated at a wooden table in a restaurant filled with working men I told Wendy and Mac of his statement. "He's like me," I said. "I'm prairie born and bred. If I'm homesick it's the place I yearn for. It's truly 'home.' I'm not like you guys, moving out to the coast with all that humidity. I like clean, clear sharp lines, dry air, brilliant sunshine. Even subzero temperatures, as long as the sky is blue."

"Enough!" cried Wendy. "You'll have Mac wanting to move back from Victoria before we are truly settled in."

"I'll drink to that," said Mac, and we toasted the Canadian flatlands.

"You're really enjoying the move, aren't you? You were saying that you've made a lot of new friends …" My voice drifted off.

"Yes," said Wendy. "It's going really well. As you know, I had to move for my health. My osteoporosis is getting worse and the cold winters aggravated it."

Mac looked pointedly at his glass of red wine. "Well," he said, "in truth, I'm still adjusting. I really love the prairies and I miss them. I miss my friends, my club …"

I took advantage of that hesitation. "Is that male bastion still operating?" His club had a reputation for chauvinism among engineers in particular.

"Yes, it is," said Wendy, "but they're older—a lot older—so the stories are more about golf than anything else."

Mac grinned ruefully. "I'm afraid she's right."

Our meal was large, heavy, and covered in gravy. The redeeming feature was the red wine, which was also big and brawny but had subtle undertones.

•   •   •

The next morning, lying there in a single bed, I marvelled at my feet. I could turn them around, move them up and down, feel the rough texture of the sheets. There was no pain! How miraculous! My prayer had been answered. I laughed out loud; two answers and only one prayer. I was on a roll!

I curled up thinking about the two French women, our laughter. We had stopped every couple of hours, taken off our boots, and massaged our feet. I remembered the texture of stone benches outside of the churches. Sometimes we each lay down on a bench, took off our boots and socks, and felt the warm and drying sun on our feet. Ecstasy! That's when time had made sense. I was just there, living and breathing. Just the moment, the talk, and my feet. The pain had not stopped but had lost its relevance.

I thought back to Kevin, my riding instructor, talking about emotional health. "If you have a vision of your life then whatever goes wrong, it's only a small part of you. You can still see the bigger picture and that gives you hope. That's emotional health. That's what you need as a rider for your mount. With a young horse there are lots of ups and downs—often just downs, at first. But the big picture keeps hope and a vision alive for the future." In my heart, I gave Kevin a hug. A wise man, and often right.

This is indeed mine, this little bit of time called life. I am the one who lives and breathes it. I can welcome others into my time and space, but it is still mine. I had a sudden image of Mac's shoulders, Wendy's back, as they had left the other morning. I remembered the recurring surge of loneliness. I had wanted to be part of their experience, included in their walk. But what really caused it? The answer went straight to my heart. I wasn't fully living in my being. I had let my world go off balance, tilting awkwardly, wanting desperately to be with others. I could feel my body respond. My heart soared and tears welled up again. It's *my* pace and it works.

My feet hit the wooden floor and I opened the shutters to look out on the main street of the little town. Below me, people stopped to talk to each other, often a baguette of bread under their arm. Someone hailed a couple, who turned, arms open, hands touching to embrace. It was the dance of the early morning. Still others hurried along, heads down, briefcases under their arms. Work was calling. I looked up at the light blue, cloudless sky. Another day of walking. *My* day to be lived!

When we met in the restaurant across from our hotel I smiled at Mac and Wendy and gave them each a hug. Wasn't it good that Wendy had decided to do this and to invite me to go with them? Wasn't that a stroke of good luck? And my accepting the invitation wasn't just a decision, but a response to a deeply felt need that I was only now beginning to understand. The cafés con leche finished, we walked out to find the arrows and start another day, each of us on our own pilgrimage, our own way.

I held the walking stick across my thighs and tapped out the rhythm as I began walking, chanting "body-mind-body-spirit-body-heart." The cadence of the walking stick and its heft in my hand were integrated into my being. I thought back to that evening in St. Jean-Pied-de-Port and the goals I had announced with such certainty—and remembered that niggling feeling that said, there's something else, something you can't yet name. From where had that feeling come? I concentrated on that moment and how I had felt. It had been in my body, deep in my stomach. I could almost put my hand on it the feeling was so strong. Before the end of my Camino, I'd name and claim that feeling. I promised myself.

⎯⎯∞⎯⎯

CHAPTER 7

THE BULLY

It was later that afternoon that Mac and I were sitting on a short stone wall in front of an albergue at the edge of the village. The sun felt hot and accusatory. I squinted out across the hills, which had been recently tilled. The lumps of clay were huge and unforgiving to cross. In their midst was a flock of sheep, oblong shapes of grey wool, spread out along the hill. Just behind them, a shepherd walked with his swag across his shoulder. He gestured to his dogs. Working like a team, they shifted the sheep to higher ground. My eyes embraced the curve of the land, the shapes of the animals.

Suddenly, a high-pitched scream shattered the silence. My breathing stopped in my gorge; my armpits prickled with sweat. It sounded like a woman being attacked! Maybe someone had taken her by surprise. Where was she? Frantically, I scanned the scene, then saw one of the shepherd's huge dogs with a small dog in his mouth.

The attacker shook his head slowly but with brutal energy. I stood frozen to the spot, listening to the victim's repeated screams. I felt the heat rise in the core of my body and spill out. I was filled with rage. "Mac," I screamed. "We've got to stop this attack! He's going to kill that little dog."

I reached down, looking for a stone. I pried one out of the roadbed, my eyes fixed in the direction of the shrieks. The moment I knelt down, I realized that the attacking dog stood taller than me. Abruptly, my courage faded. I dropped the stone and stared in horror. Mac stood, mouth open.

Suddenly, the shepherd's dog let the little dog fall from his mouth. Kayayaing in agony, it ran down the main street and disappeared around a corner, its moans audible. The massive dog loped across the field and took his place just behind the shepherd. The sheep were travelling more slowly now that they were climbing up the hill. From the distance the shepherd appeared to ignore him. A picture of servility, he followed, head hanging low, tail between his legs, abject in his obedience.

Mac started to laugh. "I saw you drop that stone, Pat. Good decision. He would have made short shrift of you!"

My mouth felt dry and sour. "You're so right, Mac," I said. "What an attack, and yet the little guy appeared unscathed. Just trauma, no injuries." We had moved into the shade of a narrow twisted tree as we talked.

"Well," said Mac, "some of the worst injuries can't be seen. I reckon he will bear a scar from today." We watched as a woman came out of her house and whistled to the dog, which scuttled inside to safety.

"We deserve a beer," I said. Wendy came up and we headed back to our *posada*, which was tucked away not far from the main street. The barman greeted us with a grunt. My Spanish had no effect on him, nor did any of our smiles.

"Not his day, I guess. He should have seen those dogs. That'd make a difference. He'd be glad to be alive." We laughed, toasted each other, and I reached into the bowl of nuts.

"I've invited Annette, the Dutch woman, to join us for the pilgrims' menu this evening," said Wendy. "She's walking on her own, like so many others, and just made the decision to stay over another night here. She's gotten tired from the pace." Wendy's face was scrunched in sympathy.

I looked at Wendy closely as she poured her beer. I walked alone, too—often for most of the day. Keeping my pace was not without its challenges. I was intrigued to see that Wendy didn't recognize that Annette and I shared challenges. Several days ago when I brought up staying overnight the idea did not even merit discussion. There was no stopping, regardless of the reason.

I took another sip of the beer, cool and bitter. I traced a pattern in the condensation on the cold surface of the glass. The drops formed around my finger. I began to make a map of my day: stopped here, walked on, passed a woman with a huge pack on the trail. The drops ran down the glass destroying the outline. I could feel the beat of my heart; the dogfight was still on my mind.

"Here comes Annette," announced Wendy. I looked up to see the tall, slender, blonde woman. She ordered a beer with us and we all leaned back against the wall of the hotel, feeling the heat and willing the sun to set.

"There's a French woman over at the albergue, Michèle de Tain," commented Annette. "She's having a tough time walking. She has macular degeneration and also Crohn's disease. I told her to join us tonight. Maybe you could speak French with her, Pat. She's finding it hard."

I had a sudden image of the older woman I'd seen earlier in the day. Her progress had been painfully slow. She would take a step, stop, then another step. Her glasses were thick and she looked ancient. When I passed her I was tempted to stop and suggest we rebalance her pack. But in the end, I reasoned that it was not my place to suggest a change when she hadn't asked for it. I was ashamed to realize that I had been glad to pass her.

"Was she carrying a huge pack?" I asked.

"I'm sure that's the same woman," said Annette.

Michèle joined us as we sat down at the table. The bartender was now our waiter. He brought the wine, plunking the carafe down on the table.

"Well now. What do you want to order?" he asked curtly, pulling the order pad from his apron.

Michèle began to explain to him that she could eat only omelettes due to her Crohn's disease. He shrugged and said laconically that the kitchen could not oblige every pilgrim who felt they wanted special treatment. He stared down at the woman; her face crumpled.

He tapped his order pad impatiently and said, "It's not on the menu, señora. You can't have one tonight. Would you like something else?" She shook her head numbly.

I listened in disbelief. So this is what Annette meant when she talked about Michèle having a bad time. A sense of outrage rose in my heart. No one should be treated this way. I thought of the little dog. Bullying raised the same fear in all of us.

I raised my voice. "Señor," I continued in Spanish, "surely you can make an omelette for this woman. She is a pilgrim. You, the Spanish, are proud of the Camino and gracious to its pilgrims. It is not reasonable that you would say 'no.' She will have an omelette." The waiter whipped around and headed out of the restaurant. The doors slammed behind him.

Michèle stared after him. "What on earth did you say to him?" she asked in surprise.

"Nothing much, but he now agrees with me," I replied.

"What did you say, Pat?" Mac asked me.

"I just told that guy that she is a pilgrim and that she wanted an omelette and that I was sure the chef was capable." I laughed dryly and so did they. The omelette arrived shortly afterwards.

"Let's get a photo of this evening," said Mac. He took out his camera.

"Señor," said the waiter, coming quickly to the table, gesturing for the camera.

"Hey," said Mac, "I think he wants to be in the picture or maybe take it for me."

"Or maybe both," I said. My dislike of the man was growing. He put his arm around Mac's shoulder and grinned into the flash.

"Just look at our guys getting their photo taken together," I said sarcastically in Spanish.

The waiter turned his dark stare on me. Between us there was a silence. His black eyes were impassive. There was no twinkle of humour or affection in them. The line of his dark eyebrows and narrow mouth framed them. He turned on his heel, looked back over his shoulder menacingly, and the restaurant door slammed behind him.

"Don't worry about him, Pat," said Michèle. "There are many like him.

I meet them all. What is more important are those who welcome me and help me as I struggle to finish the Camino before my death. They are the good ones." She turned and looked me in the eye. "My partner died two years ago. He wanted me to start the Camino sooner, but I just didn't want to leave him alone. So now, with his death, I am walking each year doing as much as I can. It isn't easy and yet I want to complete it for myself and in his memory."

She cut into the omelette. "This is so good. It's really all I can eat with my condition. Thank you for whatever you said to him. I'll send you a picture of this evening. I promise."

I felt my cheeks burn. "I'll get you another one tomorrow, Michèle," I said.

I never saw her again. But I would always carry the image of her, standing on the senda, her eyes fixed on her next step.

CHAPTER 8

A GUIDE

W e were up before sunrise the next morning. "Hope that shepherd is gone," I whispered in the dark. "I'd hate to meet that big dog today."

"Over here," whispered Wendy. "I've found the flecha." We headed down the hill while a sliver of the moon faded with the early light.

I felt the familiar surge of happiness that had accompanied me on these last few mornings of the Camino. I knew it came from the conscious anticipation of another day of living. There was a flash of silver as my bracelet caught my eye. The tiny bowl was a replica of the bowl carried by Buddhist monks that passersby fill with meagre bits of food, perhaps with just a glance. There is no choice, no asking. Just whatever comes: the day's gifts.

Slowly, the others began to walk away from me. I picked up my pace. I did not want to walk another day alone. Minutes later, my right knee began to complain. I can walk through this, I thought. I often felt discomfort in the early morning, but as my body awoke, adjusted, began to relax into the day, the pain disappeared almost like a bad dream.

Ten minutes later the pain was worse. I was walking too fast again. I thought back to my insight with Jeanne and Katie. My pace was as unique as my passport, like an identity card. I could not deny it. I could change it at my own risk. I could freely love, admire, respect, know it for what it meant to each moment of my journey. Listening to the voice in my head, I realized that loving my pace would not come easily. All my life I had longed to be a full-fledged member of the group, to walk step by step with friends and companions. I could see that my pace had defined me, determining my context.

As I reflected on this, my mind turned again to Coelho and his advice. His reaction to complex challenges went beyond the exercises for daily meditation. Curious, I stopped and searched my backpack for the pages I had ripped from his book. They were stuffed into a side pocket. I smoothed them out and began to read.

He pointed out that each of us has a guide on the Camino whose duty is to comfort, support, and ease us through the challenging lessons encountered daily on the Camino, lessons that would beg logic and experience.

The challenge was how to visualize and contact the guide. First Coelho described clearly what the process would produce. The guide's face would appear framed between two walls of flames, an alleyway between them. Next he explained how to create the scenario. First, visualize high flames on the left. In your imagination, stoke the flames until they burn consistently. Then turn your attention to the right side and repeat the process. Do not lose contact with the wall of fire on the left. Leave the alleyway open between as he suggested. Your product is the image of two "hedges" of flames, burning brightly along a central alley. Look deeply inward. When you have established communication, ask your guide to become visible to you. Coelho promises the guide will appear when called.

I started with the first step he suggested. I visualized a wall of fire on my left. It spluttered and died. I breathed deeply and focused. This time it took the form of dazzling red flames. Hypnotized, I rested my gaze on their movement, then I visualized the same wall of flames to my right. Next, I stoked both of them; the flames moved nervously, their reach was low. Finally, the fire caught and leapt to the skies. Between the walls of flames, just as Coelho had said, a face appeared. The shape was blurred, but the eyes, which gazed deeply into mine, were wise and loving. I had seen those eyes before.

"You are where you should be. This is your life to lead. You have as much time as you need, but you too will die when your quest is finished. Do not be afraid; I will be with you." The soft brown eyes did not smile. They looked deep inside me.

Had I really hear those words? I couldn't remember. They seemed organic, to have grown in me. The feeling of comfort and of being understood was overwhelming. I breathed into a spot just below the bellyband of my pack, a place of energy and strength. I looked around. I was standing beside a small grove of trees and rocks and had the uncomfortable feeling of being watched. I peered into the trees. There was no one there.

How long have I been standing here, I wondered. Feeling silly, I started to walk, counting my steps and watching the time on my watch. The guide's presence remained with me, more as a sense of peace than a guide. I walked down the ditch to cross a major freeway.

On the other side a small bus was parked close to the road barrier. I looked inside as I passed. The bus was full of backpacks, suitcases, and coats. A short way along the track I heard people talking. Turning the corner, I came upon a large group dressed for a walk in the city. Some carried packs, but many didn't. They all had walking sticks and used them with authority. Listening closely I could make out words of their conversations. They were German speaking. As I drew up to them, they turned and hailed me. One of the men introduced himself. Like the others, he was German Catholic and part of an annual trip to walk another part of the Camino.

"Are you walking all of it?" I asked, curious. He explained that they chose only the parts of great historical or religious significance. This year, they would stop at Burgos and León, for example, to see the cathedrals.

I listened critically to their choices. They had travelled by bus and so had less contact with significant aspects of the Camino. They chose to visit only cathedrals of some note. Yet, in my experience, the small churches, with their statues of the Virgin and their bas-reliefs of daily life, gave a glimpse of how the church had lived with its parishioners and now with its passersby. As Christians, they had missed opportunities to understand this.

"And you," he said. "Where are you from? Why are you walking it?" As I told my story, the others dropped back and listened.

"Such a distance to come," said one of the women. She turned to the others and said something in German. Everyone smiled.

As I turned to follow the next bend in the road, the group held up their walking sticks to form an arch and cheered as I passed beneath it. I looked back at them, embarrassed. They held the arch high for several more pilgrims just behind me.

"See you again," I called out to them as I left.

Swinging my walking stick, I reflected on the last few days. I had a growing sense of how the Camino brought all of its pilgrims together in a common understanding of our humanity. Each of us had our reason for walking, our sense of purpose, our fears, dreams, and support. In spite of my walking on my own I was never alone in the act of walking. Across the ages—now and forever—as long as there was a Camino, we would walk and learn about ourselves and our way of being in the world.

•   •   •

It was late in the afternoon when I reached Viana. Wendy and Mac were sitting at an outside table in front of a small restaurant. I pulled up another plastic bar chair, took off my pack, and stretched out my legs.

"God, it feels good to take the weight off," I said, letting my body slump, my shoulders relax. "This is one helluva long walk." We looked at each other for a split second and burst into laughter. I took the beer from the waiter who came up to us, then ordered some tapas.

"So how was your day?" asked Mac.

Scenes flashed on my mind's eye: churches, fields, and groups of pilgrims. Emotions of fatigue, loneliness, and serenity flooded into different parts of my body. I looked around the bar and then back at them.

"It was a great day. Lots of experiences," I said. "Just so beautiful." There was a moment's pause. It lengthened.

"How was yours?" I asked, looking from one to the other. They glanced briefly at each other.

"Oh, it was fine. We've been here for over an hour though," answered Wendy. "Do you have any idea how much we worry about you? I'm sure also," she added bitterly, "that everyone wonders why you are walking alone." Her eyes flashed, her jaw set and her teeth clenched. The line of her lips was jagged and harsh. Her eyes fixed on mine in accusation.

"Well," I said. "Don't. Worrying is a futile activity. If there's anything wrong—"

Mac interrupted me. "But you might have met another pervert. How would we know? Look what happened at the playground. You were so alone. And it happened so suddenly."

"So alone," added Wendy.

"Well," I began, "that's how it is with me. I am alone sometimes. Not always because I walk slowly, but I also—"

This time Wendy interrupted. "I'm sure everyone thinks we're terrible for not waiting for you. It's just that …" She stopped. "Well, we walk faster than you do."

"It's okay, Wendy." I set my glass down a little harder than I realized. The beer sloshed on the table. "We've already talked about pace. We talked in Calgary. We've talked here. We all agree. We stick to our pace. When …" The conversation with the Swiss came back to mind. "If anyone asks why I am walking alone, I just tell them we have different paces. They accept that. Look, the most important thing is that we've agreed how to handle it. So it's not a problem."

Mac looked at me solemnly. Wendy whirled her wine glass on the wet table. I sipped my beer, which tasted wonderful—so cool, so wonderfully wet and sharp.

"Well, there is something, though, that we might talk about." I felt my courage sinking into my boots. "I really wish we'd have lunch or coffee somewhere on the—"

"Yeah, but if we do that we are so late getting into the last town." Wendy's voice was shrill.

"Sure, you're right," I said quickly. "No problem." My inner voice said, "Liar."

That night dinner was in an elegant restaurant, a rare treat. We arrived early in case there were lots of people. We found ourselves in a large empty dining room. There was one other table of pilgrims. The maître d' stood at the back of the room near the doors leading to the kitchen. His serviette hung from the front of his belt. His arms were crossed and he scowled at us. We smiled at him and sat at the only table with a couple of pilgrims.

One of the men reached out to shake hands with us. "I'm Pierre-Yves," he said. "I come from Quebec, the city of Quebec. I am glad to meet other *canadiens*." He pointed to the maple leaf pinned on Mac's collar. His smile was warm.

"Why are you doing the Camino, Pierre-Yves?" asked Mac.

"Well, I am … 'ow do you call it … doing a *pèlerinage*?" He looked around the table for help.

"Pilgrimage," I translated.

"Ah, oui, of course, pilgrimage. I have lost some of my faith. I am wanting to find it again." His accent was the taste of home. His bright brown eyes moved from one person to the other, searching for connections.

Our meal finished much later and our conversation came to an end. Several other tables were filled now. The Swiss were intensely involved in a conversation in French at one table. At another table I saw Marie Claire, a woman from Algeria whom I had met on day one. She was laughing with a swarthy man whose accent was Mediterranean. A Belgian named Jean-Baptiste introduced himself and pushed his table back to talk to Geoff who was nearby.

Mac looked around the room, puzzled. "Pat, you speak French, why is it that they have so much fun? They're always joking around. What are they talking about?"

I looked at his earnest face, short hair, and the clean shirt he had put on for dinner. "Well, Mac, it's not so much what they are talking about but rather what they aren't talking about."

"So, what's that mean?" asked Wendy.

"They never talk about what they are going to do in the morning. Tonight, for example, before we got to the restaurant we had scoped out the walk for tomorrow, where we'd end, what the history of those twenty-five kilometres is. We did all of that. They just get up, face west, and start walking. One foot in front of the other—that's their plan. When the group—or someone—is tired, they stop, have a couple of drinks, laugh, hang out together. They don't plan so there's no plan to stick to. It's that infamous word, 'spontaneous.'" I heard the truth in what I said and started to laugh. They hesitated, looking at me intensely, then laughed along with me.

A slender grey-haired man at a nearby table turned and smiled at us. "Sounds as though you're enjoying your evening," he commented. His two younger companions pulled their chairs closer to our table.

"I'm Charles," he said holding out his hand, "and this is my daughter Mary and her friend Dora. I saw you earlier today. Where are you from?"

"Pull up closer," said Mac. "We're from Canada. Let's have a glass of wine together before we call it a night."

Dora stood up quickly. "I'm off, Mary, Charles. See you in the morning."

"We're doing this pilgrimage together, Mary and me." Charles continued. "She's just finished her medical degree and—"

"Yes," she interrupted. "Dad wanted us to spend some time together. I'm following in his footsteps—as a doctor and on this Camino."

He smiled at her, his eyes crinkled. I noticed then that he was thin, almost frail. His face was drawn and grey. I leaned forward to hear him better.

"It's not your usual way to spend time," he commented. "But we both like to walk and so—"

"And," Mary interrupted again, "if I can get him to take it a little easier, we'll finish together, too." She looked worried. "I start at Dad's alma mater a week after we finish this." She reached over and hugged him.

"No need to overdo this, Mary," he snapped. "I'll be around for a few years yet." Her eyes filled with tears and she pulled away.

• • •

The sun had set, leaving a deep blue sky dotted with white shimmering clouds. I felt the night air soft on my face. The three of us were sitting together across from Viana's Hotel Casa Armendariz enjoying the perfection of the evening. The waiter had just set two snifters of cognac and an empty glass in front of us.

"This is perfect," I said with a sigh. "I can't imagine a place I would rather be, or for that matter people I would rather be with." I lifted my glass and poured some cognac into the empty glass for Wendy. Mac did the same.

"They consistently overestimate how much we can drink," said Wendy as she clinked her glass against mine.

"It's the right side to err on, though," said Mac with a smile.

I stretched my legs out, admiring my black silk slacks. "Just look at your dress, Wendy. They must do something with this silk. We have no creases."

"True, but then who would ever notice?" she asked.

A comfortable silence spread between us. A group of young people suddenly ran into the square laughing and calling out to each other. Some were wearing backpacks and carrying their pilgrim sticks. Their energy filled the space and followed them down the street toward the albergue. The noise lingered and then finally faded.

"What were the high points for you today?" asked Wendy, twirling her glass as she looked from Mac to me.

"What I'm loving," said Mac as he folded his hands under his chin, "is the sheer pleasure of covering the kilometres at my own pace and in my own time. We're all active and I love to walk a lot. But this is my first experience with walking as my sole means of getting around. And I can even predict with some accuracy where I'll be and how long it will take. I'm getting stronger, too. I can feel it."

Wendy continued twirling her glass. I tilted my head back and watched the early stars appearing on the horizon. The silence lengthened. "For me," she said softly, "it's what I see in our fellow pilgrims and in the people we encounter along the way. And, really, in us, too. There is something special …" She stopped. "That's not the right word. It's more than that. It's as though we have some bigger part of us that we've caught a glimpse of now and then. And it becomes clearer as I walk. I have the feeling that the walking is how our mind and our heart are tied together. Or maybe they are embedded in our body and walking makes it obvious. What do you think?"

She looked at me. Suddenly, I felt connected to both of them at a depth that surprised me. We might not spend days walking together yet our experiences had much in common. At the core of the walking was our connection to the Camino.

"I think I share that feeling, Wendy." I heard a tentative note in my voice. "I have been thinking that the body is home for all of our experiences, our thoughts, our soul—if we have one. And I've asked myself if I am thinking this way because I've—we've—been walking for days now. I had a random thought about the Bible and Moses today. Do you remember his story? He spent forty days and nights alone on the mountain. And in the end he had gained huge insights—truths that he spoke about to the others."

"That's an interesting case in point," Mac laughed. "I don't remember why Moses was doing time, but I'm not."

"Not so fast, Mac," Wendy interrupted. "I remember from one of my lit courses that forty is a key number in the Bible. Often it's about someone being tested for forty days and then, at the end, there is a time of renewal—or transformation, or whatever you want to call it. It may prove to be the same for us. By the time we've finished it'll be likely thirty-five or thirty-six days."

"Just listen to us talk! Do you remember that first night in St. Jean-Pied-de-Port when we shared our goals? Nothing we said that night would ever have predicted this conversation." I lifted my glass. "Here's to us!"

Geoff and Sebastian appeared suddenly and joined us at the table. I sat listening to the banter and joining in the laughter. In my silence were the stories of my guide, my meditation, about how the Camino was shifting and shaping my being in the world. I felt torn. Why not share right now? What was holding me back? Puzzled, I took another sip of cognac and swirled my glass around the unspoken words. As I turned inward I became aware again of a shapeless form that hid in my being. There was no pressure to share now. There would be time enough. I'll stay true to the need to gain clarity in my thoughts and to follow my own sense of timing, I reasoned.

We walked back to our hotel, which was just off one of the main streets. Whispering "good night" Geoff and Sebastian left us and headed for the albergue. We pulled on the bell hanging beside the ornate, medieval wooden doors. True to the style of these doors, there was a wrought iron grill at eye level. We heard steps, the grill slid open, and an eye peered out at us.

There was a short silence, the bolt rattled, and the door opened. I stepped over the threshold into the dimly lit passageway. I could barely make out the size of the space. An ominous feeling of being betwixt and between, of not being real, caught in my throat. This must be when the travellers of old wrote: "Here there be dragons" on maps where there was no clear way to navigate, no signs, and no guides. No one had gone there before. We stopped, stood still, as the night watchman's keys rattled.

"Is this where our rooms are?" My voice sounded hollow.

"Yeah. We left our packs in the rooms," replied Mac right behind me.

I shivered and peered into the darkness wishing we had never left the well-lit plaza. I experienced a formless anxiety. I knew something would happen. Then the door opened and the watchman turned to let us pass. I looked up at the arch above the passageway and caught sight of a horseshoe hanging there. For me, horseshoes had always been a symbol of power and protection, an invitation to go forward with confidence.

"What an eerie experience," said Wendy as she walked into the hallway leading to our rooms.

"It's September 22, the equinox," I reminded them. "Remember, the Celts believed that the veils between the worlds were thinnest during the solstice and that magic was afoot. I agree with them. And this evening it seems that magic is part of the equinox, too."

The watchman gave us keys and left on silent feet. I curled up, blankets pulled around my ears. I listened to my breathing, searched the darkness. I could see nothing that inspired confidence. Morning could not come too soon.

CHAPTER 9

BELIEVING

The restaurant was full of early morning noises: people talking, calling out to each other, and ordering breakfast. We found a table in a corner and Mac pulled out his map and guidebook. A silence fell over us as he began.

"I see it this way. We have about ten kilometres to walk to Logroño and everyone is saying that the festival is worth seeing. We can do that easily and spend time enjoying the town, catch up with David and Marion. Maybe take in some bullfights and some bars. We likely need a change of pace and activities." He stopped and looked at us.

Mac continued his scope and sequence. "We'll make up time the day after that. The distance to Nájera is nearly thirty kilometres."

"Time to hit the road," I said, reaching for my pack. "I'll see you in Logroño."

We all turned on the road heading west out of town. Before long, I was trailing them. It's a ritual, I thought. Even if I changed walking companions I'd drop behind.

I sank into my body, sensing the rhythm, the sheer pleasure of walking. I picked up my stick and held it in both hands just in front of my legs. As it bumped rhythmically against my thighs I began my chant: "body-mind-body-spirit-body-heart." I looked back over my shoulder to take in the early morning sky with its shades of pink, silver, and gold. The clouds were round and shone with golden light against the high blue. How blessed I felt.

As I thought of my good blessings, I felt a movement on my left. To my great surprise, my paint horse, Indio, appeared to walk beside me. He turned his head and our gazes met. The sun caught his solitary mystic blue eye and it flashed in my direction. I could feel his soft warm breath on my hand. Then there was movement on my right. I turned to see Prince, the first horse I had ever owned, his neck arched, feet moving freely above the cobblestones. My heart swelled with love for them. They were constant companions all morning, following me willingly over the cobblestones and along the road.

How to make sense of last night's deep anxiety when it had evaporated so easily with this euphoric morning? I walked farther, thinking of the contrasts between the days. Today, I felt so grounded in my world. I smiled. Didn't the word "grounded" appeal to a sense of reality? How could I call this grounded when I saw and experienced my horses as though they were real, walking beside me? I felt a new surge of happiness at their being with me in spirit if not in body.

It was true that happiness had a draw for everyone. But without anxiety, would I truly understand happiness? I doubted it. Happiness and anxiety were two end points on a continuum. Together they formed the context for understanding both emotions. Without that context something would be lost in my everyday appreciation of these emotions. On this trip I had lived with both.

How could Indio and Prince appear so real? Where had they come from? They were not part of any physical reality. Was my imagination that strong? This was the first time I had experienced such vivid companions. How could I make sense of it?

Baffled, I continued walking, tapping my thighs and chanting again. I could visualize the two points of the walking stick and how they defined each other and set up a context. As I looked at my stick I wondered at what point anxiety or groundedness stopped? Or started? What happened in the middle—wherever it was?

Then I remembered an article on the meaning of paradox by Parker J. Palmer that I had used in a lecture. He had said that opposites don't negate each other; they come together in a mysterious unity. He went on to say that they needed each other to create meaning. It was the space between the well-lit plaza and the dark, inside threshold that had put fear into me. Perhaps it was this kind of space that opened up the possibility for the horses to walk with me. It gave me permission to reconstruct, align, and understand reality differently. I continued walking and recalled something I had read years ago about liminal space: a space that is neither up nor down, in nor out, real nor imagined. It was the space beyond the world we knew. I shivered. That was what I was experiencing—something beyond the world I knew.

The sun climbed in the sky and the midday grew hot. I filled my water bottle at a well in a small town, chatting with the locals, and then headed off without taking a break. The heat beat down.

As I reached the outskirts of Logroño, the traffic increased and the merrymakers appeared with noisemakers and wearing scarves and shirts with the crest of Logroño. I spotted Wendy and Mac sitting in a small bar waving at me. I dropped my pack beside them and slid into a chair.

"Does look like a fête tonight," commented Mac.

"What's happened to our Aussies?" I asked.

"We saw them a while ago just as we arrived. They'll join us at seven in the central plaza," Wendy replied. "They are checking into a refugio and freshening up."

We began walking along the street. Traffic had been shut down and the roads were crowded with celebrants, beer in hand. We walked along, laughing and talking in Spanish and English to anyone who engaged us.

"This is how we should learn second languages," said Mac. "If I had had these opportunities, I'd be fluent."

"That's why I ran trips to Quebec," I said. "What a student of language needs is an attitude of wanting to understand—especially at first—rather than a lot of vocabulary and verb tenses."

A handsome man ran up to me. His eyes were bright and shiny and his beer was sloshing in his hand. He said something in rapid-fire Spanish and threw his arm around my waist, then waltzed me several steps, planted a kiss on my cheek, and staggered on down the street.

"Case in point," laughed Wendy.

We turned into a plaza where there were lanterns strung and tables set with bright tablecloths. The crowd was a mixture of families with children, couples, tables of men or women. The buzz of voices was inviting and we sat near one of the doors so that David and Marion would easily find us.

"This looks like a Matisse painting," said Wendy.

I began talking to the couple at the table beside ours and asked them about the bullfights.

"What a pity," said the man. "Not many tourists really want to see them anymore. They finished tonight about an hour ago."

I turned and translated for Wendy and Mac. At that moment, David and Marion started to move through the crowd heading for our table. I felt a momentary annoyance. Why couldn't they spend an evening without us? I looked at their smiling faces and air of anticipation. Don't be such a grouch, I reminded myself sourly. It's been three nights.

"Where are you folks from? The US?" asked my neighbour.

"No, señor," I replied. "Somos canadienses. From the west." They both lit up and said that they had visited Canada and how beautiful they found our country.

David's voice cut in abruptly, "Come on, Pat! I haven't had a hug yet." I turned and saw him, arms open, smiling. I stood up, moved around the table and gave him a huge hug, my conversation interrupted. So, catching the eye of my Spanish neighbour, I said, "Excuse me, señor. Perhaps we'll have another opportunity later?"

Now that David and Marion had sat down our table swung into English. We ordered our dinners, a bottle of wine, and some dessert. The talking, laughing, and greeting friends continued around us. I watched the flashing black eyes, children misbehaving, and adults ignoring them.

"This is really an atmosphere of carnival," said Mac. "No holds barred."

It was well past midnight when we returned to our hotel. David and

Marion waved and headed for their refugio. We promised to meet at seven to start our long day of more than thirty kilometres. As I climbed the stairs I realized that the streets were still full. I found the party noises strangely comforting as I eased into sleep.

. . .

The neon numbers of the alarm shone in the darkness. I looked around cautiously and saw that the room was as ordinary as I remembered it. There was a chair against the wall, two night tables, the half-opened door to the shower. Nothing recalled the sense of being out of step with reality that I had been feeling off and on for the last couple of days. I slumped back on the bed. My energy was so low and I had awoken with the familiar tightness in my throat. What kept provoking this lingering sadness? It clung to me like a shadow and nothing got rid of it.

I thought back over our days of walking. There had been moments when the desire to sob out loud had been overwhelming. Sometimes it happened first thing in the morning; other times it occurred at the end of the day, when I longed to share my thoughts and experiences. Or when I was talking at the table, sharing a cognac. I couldn't find any reason for these feelings in the day's events or relationships.

I pulled on my boots and made sure there was nothing left in the room. My pack bumped the wall several times as I walked down into the restaurant. The two couples called out to me when I arrived. We chatted for a few moments as I waited for coffee and then we headed for the door one after the other in a straight line. Outside the darkness was thick and the horizon inky black. We were slightly earlier than usual. The daily search for the flecha ended immediately when David called, "Over here, you guys. This is it." The day's walk had begun.

Determined to spend the day in good spirits, I sought out other resources that had sustained me. These had come into my life as part of deep, spiritual experiences. Or if not spiritual, they were beyond logical explanation—as was my guide—and based on moments of colour and movement.

I called up the wolf, my totemic animal. But it was fruitless. He was beyond my call. His image flashed on my inner eye, disappeared, then flashed again. It lacked strength and staying power.

I set my pace, swung the stick with rhythm, and watched the sunrise crack the blackness. I continued with this pace, feeling my strength and my sense of purpose returning. The sense of dislocation lifted. I turned to my guide, whom I had named Estragon, stroking the flames that framed his face. He was unresponsive today and appeared only briefly.

For the first hours of the day I walked with a deep sense of rhythm that blocked all concerns for time and pace. The dusty toes of my hiking boots appeared and disappeared with a regularity that was hypnotic. The sounds of the walking stick were like a soft percussion accompaniment. At one point, I remembered an equestrian instructor telling me that I should cast my gaze forward and hook my eyes on the horizon and draw the horse and me to it. Looking down, she explained, turned my energy inward and left my horse fretting about the lack of direction.

I raised my eyes and followed the rounded shoulders of the hills. The geometric patterns of fields, roads, and pastures marked out by stone fences mesmerized me. They filled a space in my core where I longed to stay. It was as though a huge, three-dimensional Vasarely had been constructed by the landscape and I had the privilege of being able to sink into its depths and contemplate all its perspectives.

I arrived in Navarrete by midday under a cloudless sky with a finger of heat pointing at the back of my neck. Pilgrims had filled their water bottles and were now sitting in the shade of trees near the fountain in the plaza. I heard the sounds of French and sat down near the small group.

"Eh, well, so we are all Canadian then?" I asked. The man who answered me was tall, dark haired, and wore a straw hat. The rim was stained with sweat.

"Me, yes. But you, no. If an accent means anything!" He grinned as he said it. They were from Quebec, from Lac St. Jean specifically, and had started walking just south of Paris. As we chatted they recommended that

I visit the Iglesia de la Asunción, which had a remarkable baroque retablo. I nodded in agreement. They stood up, bundled their packs tightly, and walked off into the glare of the sun.

I sat enjoying the shade and listening to conversations around me. I could see the church tower and I knew that I should go and view the famous altarpiece. The heat had sunk into my body and sweat poured down. Finally, I stood up, checked my pack, and headed toward the yellow arrow, out of town. I walked past the iglesia but didn't stop. There would be magnificent paintings and retablos in Burgos where we'd be in a couple of days.

The trail out of town was not heavily travelled. It wended its way along vineyards and farms before turning onto a gravel road. The French Canadians were long out of sight and I was walking alone. I looked at the grapes, which were ripe. Some of them had likely gone into the wines at the festival in Logroño. I was about to stop and rebalance my pack, when I saw a lone man walking. There was no sign of a car or other people. What on earth was he doing out here? He certainly wasn't dressed like a pilgrim. I felt a sudden flash of fear. As we drew closer my grip tightened on my walking stick. Then he smiled and said, "Buen Camino." My intuition reminded me that I had nothing to fear, to relax. I kept up my pace as I passed and nodded at him. It was another hundred metres farther before I took a deep breath and let go of the fear. Soon after that the road took a right-angle turn around a stand of grape vines and I saw a red car with a small dog on the front seat. It was most likely his and he was inspecting the vineyards.

My walking stick was now swinging loosely in my hand. How could I keep fear in balance when I was in so many new situations and so much was unpredictable? Predicting is so focused on being in control of situations, on being safe. It emphasizes the negatives: fear and shutting down. Given my experience with the exhibitionist and being totally alone then—and now for that matter—how could I be open to situations like today where there had been nothing to fear?

My thoughts turned to Indio and the fear I had felt when I started riding him as a young horse. I remembered him bucking down a steep ridge, Kevin shouting, "Stop him!" Yet he had been dependable in other situations. The day we got tangled in barbwire he had stopped as soon as I said "whoa" and stood still while I untangled us. Yet I could see that my trust was contained by fear and uncertainty. What would happen if I trusted him? He had earned more trust than I gave him. What if I closed the book on fear? What happened in relationships where trust was the norm?

When I arrived in Nájera late that afternoon the pedestrian street was crowded with people. I spotted Wendy and Mac at a round table covered with tapas and empty wine glasses. I flopped down, setting my pack by the wall.

"Where are David and Marion?" I asked, gesturing to the evidence.

"They headed off for a rest," said Wendy. "But we have an unopened bottle of wine and some cheese if you'd like to sample it and see the rooms we've rented."

"That was another heck of a long walk!" I announced, getting up from the table. "If there's one thing that would make it seem worthwhile a glass of wine would likely be it. Let's go!" I picked up my pack and we paid the waiter who was at the back of the bar enjoying the coolness.

We crossed the plaza, wending our way among the crowds of men and women carrying string bags filled with fruit and vegetables. The door to the hotel was at the back of a restaurant. We started climbing up to the second floor where Mac and Wendy had booked rooms.

"I was thinking again today how we underestimated the length of this walk. It needs spiritual comforts—pun intended!" I looked over my shoulder.

Mac grinned wryly. "Isn't innocence a gift? Do you think we'd still be walking if we had started out knowing how tough it would get?"

"Fortunately, we'll never know," I said with deep conviction. "How was your day?"

"Do you want to tell Pat, Mac?" asked Wendy.

"Well, yes, I want us to have a glass of wine and talk about it together, the three of us," said Mac, and he looked at me. I returned his glance, raising my eyebrow.

"Nothing serious," he assured me. "No crisis."

We opened the bottle and spread the cheese on a bit of paper towel. Wendy and I leaned back on the pillows and Mac sat at the end of the double bed.

There was a moment of awkward silence as he poured the wine. Wendy held up her glass as a toast.

"Well," Mac began. "You'll remember that there was a short walk off to a monastery? It was only a few kilometres off the trail and I figured I had enough time to take it and still catch up to you. No problem."

"Slight bit of male ego," Wendy interrupted. "And that's why I didn't go along. Too much muscle and not enough reflection." When I looked at her, I saw how dark her eyes were and how concerned. Curious, I thought.

Mac's expression didn't change. "So I could see it on the hill to the south. Didn't look far and I just picked up my pace. It was a steady climb but not steep. There was no one else around so I was really aware of the silence and the solitude. A lot like you were the other day, Pat."

I nodded. I remembered our long talk about that. I looked again at Wendy whose eyes were focused intently on Mac's face.

"I was close to the summit when I saw him."

"I thought you were walking alone?" I reminded him.

"So did I. But no. He was a tall man, my height, wearing a long, grey garment, like a priest's robe. The hood was covering part of his face. He was striding along, but carrying a walking stick that he used to navigate the rocky part of the path in front of me. I said, "Buen Camino," but he didn't answer me. It was his lack of reply that made me feel there was something strange about this man. He seemed somehow familiar. Then it hit me. It was me."

Mac looked down; I saw his knuckles tighten on the wine glass. There was a silence in the room. Wendy turned the wine glass in her hand.

"What do you mean, it was you?" I queried in disbelief.

"It was me. I was old—likely about eighty years old—an old man. But I'm sure it was me. It was as though someone gave me a window on the future and how I'd be in it." Mac didn't take his eyes off my face. I stared back at him. The conviction in his voice, the look on his face was compelling.

Wendy met my eyes. "I'm convinced that's what—no, who—he saw, Pat. We've had a long talk and I feel it more each time he talks about it. It's another experience of the spiritual kind—like the kind you've had, too."

I looked at them. Why wouldn't it be true? When I told them about Indio walking along with me they accepted my story, as bizarre as it was. As I sat there it dawned on me that it was the reality I had conveyed that convinced them, not logic or argument. And I had assumed they would just accept my story, my reality, without question. It was the essence of believing Mac's story, too.

"You know, Mac," I said. "I believe you. Whatever this walk is and has been for millennia, for us it has opened up our understanding of who we are and how we live our lives—of how many realities we are a part of. And it has always done that. You met yourself coming down from the summit. You are who you are now and who you are in the future—and I reckon your past is always in you, too. Why wouldn't you see and feel your life in all its realities? Walk in them?"

I poured the wine and Wendy cut up more of the cheese. Our silence filled the room and the spaces between us. It was a lively silence, full of portent and meaning. How would the rest of our days go? What was in store for us? Would anyone else ever understand our transformations? Suddenly, I felt the familiar fear and apprehension flow through my veins. I saw us standing on a precipice about to take the next step into a void.

"Time for a shower and then another gourmet dinner," I announced, laughing as I stood up, all the while knowing I had moved too quickly, that the conversation was cut off before its time.

———❈———

CHAPTER 10

CONVERSATIONS

The restaurant was full of noisy talk, laughter, and the clash of cutlery against plates and bowls. After we squeezed in beside David and Marion and a German-speaking man, we turned to the task of eating, passing bowls of noodles and ordering bottles of wine. I looked around the table at the suntanned faces, felt the exuberance in the air, and marvelled at how quickly we fixated on food.

"So, how was your day, Pat?" Marion asked. I launched into a description of the day, but in the back of my mind I watched how quickly I dropped the image of Mac and the old man meeting on the road. That story and this reality were so divorced, yet both were very real.

As we stood up to make room for the next group of pilgrims, I overheard someone say, "Yes, in its heyday, it was one of the great churches for Gregorian chant." I turned and saw two pilgrims deep in conversation. I went over to the end of the long table where they were seated.

"By any chance are you talking about the church just across the plaza?" I asked.

The tall, angular, blonde woman looked up at me. "As a matter of fact, yes," she said. "They'll be singing there in about a half hour. I'm headed over."

"Are you interested?" I asked my friends excitedly. "To hear Gregorian chant in an old church would be a dream come true—one I never thought would happen in my life. It'll be even better because it isn't a scheduled concert. It's just one of the moments in the daily life of a Catholic church—as it's been since time immemorial." I looked eagerly at them. David and Marion looked at each other.

"We may give it a miss, Pat," said David. "We are Church of England, you know. Not really interested in the RC experience."

"But it's not …" I started, and then changed my mind. As a child I had listened to Gregorian chant on an old radio that I used to hide beneath the covers. The beauty of the deep male voices had held me in its spell then and I loved it still.

"We'll come along, Pat," said Mac. I smiled at him and Wendy. It would be good to have company. We stopped at the little bar nearby for our post dinner cognac before walking over to the main portal of the church. When we arrived, there were several statues of saints at the door, and as we entered I noticed statues above it as well. In medieval times, this space—between the carnal world and its sins and the place of worship—was considered a prime liminal space where danger lurked. The statues and holy water were there to protect believers the moment they entered the church.

The lighting was soft inside the tiny, ancient church; shadows deep in the recesses of the walls partially hid the Stations of the Cross. The statue of the Virgin Mary stood behind the altar to the left.

We sat down in the front pew. There were a few pilgrims whom I recognized, but the church was basically empty. I got up and went over to the stand where tall, narrow candles flickered and wax had dripped on the floor. I struck a match and lit a candle in memory of my parents. As I sat down, Wendy whispered, surprise in her voice, "Are you Catholic?"

I smiled at her. "No, not even a little. That was a symbolic gesture. In memory of my parents."

"So, your parents were churchgoers?"

"Not even. When I was young we rarely went to church—and if we did, it was to the United Church. By the time I was twelve or thirteen, my parents stopped attending altogether. They just talked to my brother and me about leading a good Christian life."

"I'm not sure I get it," said Wendy.

"I'm not surprised. It took me a while. They had no respect for the hypocrisy they found in churches. On the other hand their belief in God was so deep and their faith in souls going to heaven was unshakeable. They didn't need sermons on Sunday. In their mind, the evidence of God's existence was in the beauty of nature and the goodness they found in others."

I smiled at Wendy who shrugged her shoulders then focused on the altar. We continued waiting in the silence for the priest to come and give us his blessings before the singing would begin. The smell of incense and the lingering presence of tired bodies permeated the church. Slowly, pilgrims arrived until there was little room left.

The priest who walked up to the altar was not young. His gestures were rituals of long practice and his Spanish flowed seamlessly through the mass. He accepted each participant, gave absolution, and finally turned to hold the goblet high toward the cross behind the altar. He then asked us, his audience, to stand and receive his blessing as he called out place names across the world. At the end, he asked those whose homes had been missed to stand and share them with us.

There was a moment's silence as he left and then we heard the deep voices of men begin the Gregorian chant. The first priest appeared through a door near the choir stalls followed by two others. The first two men were grey haired; the last one frail and bent with age. The chant was without time and the church resonated with its purity. It drew me along as though I were on a timeless path so deep that form and substance were without meaning. It came to me suddenly that this was what Rumi was talking about when he said there was a unified field beyond the duality of good and evil, one we embrace into our lives without study.

We walked back slowly to the Monasterio de Santa Teresa without talking. In the silence, I embraced an overwhelming sense of peace that arose in me. We rang the bell and a nun in traditional habit appeared. Her long skirts moved gently as she closed the door behind us and wished us good night.

The next morning, David and Marion were eating breakfast when
we arrived at the restaurant. David was wearing his straw hat with corks
around the rim. They swung drunkenly as he turned his head and dunked
his croissant in the coffee.

"So how was the church thing?" he asked.

"It was fascinating," said Wendy. "Only three singers but a beautiful
sound."

"Everyone back home says that the Catholic Church is losing
attendance. No idea why that's happened." Marion smiled primly as she cut
up an orange.

I felt a flash of annoyance. "What goes around, comes around," I
said pointedly. "In your place, I wouldn't take the large attendance in the
Church of England for granted."

The silence was framed by the sounds of coffee being drunk and
knives cutting on plates. After a moment, I looked over at Wendy. "I think
one of the reasons people attend church less frequently is obvious. Did you
notice the bas-reliefs along the walls as we walked out? They are scenes of
everyday life. Animals, shepherds, fields, workers—all the earth's creatures
playing their part in ordinary events, like reaping and sowing."

Wendy nodded her head in agreement and gestured with her coffee
cup to Mac. He got up and went over to the counter.

"So when I wonder about why the church no longer reached out to
the common man, I think of the later bas-reliefs that focused on saints.
The cathedrals lost their common touch. Rather than scenes of everyday
working life, the bas-relief was ornate, painted gold, peopled with saints
and devoted to an abstract you couldn't see or feel."

Wendy looked over at Mac and asked for milk. Mac drank his coffee,
his head bent, eyes lowered. I looked at him, then at Wendy. The silence
continued, broken only by the occasional slurp of coffee.

Looking around the table but making eye contact with Wendy only,
I continued, "I think the church lost touch not only with the common
man but also with the Biblical stories. Believers had an emotional need
to belong, to be touched with grace. Yet the church offered so little

validation and recognition. Why didn't the RC church—or some other institution for that matter—bridge the gap?"

The silence stretched out, long and uninterrupted. I looked at them seriously, letting the silence hang. David nodded to Marion, who stood up and shook the crumbs off her slacks.

"Well," said Mac as he got up, "I think it's time to make a move. Let's leave in ten minutes."

"You're on, mate," said David, grinning. "See you down here shortly."

I rearranged my bag and swung it on my back. It's early in the day for this kind of esoteric talk, I thought to myself.

I stepped out into the darkness and breathed in the soft morning air. A large yellow arrow signalled the route out of town and several groups of pilgrims headed purposefully toward it. Finally, the door behind me opened and I heard familiar voices.

"There you are, Pat," said David. "I was wondering if you'd left us behind!"

"Not likely, mate," I replied as we started to walk and our daily pattern emerged. Wendy and Mac were together in the lead, followed closely by David, and several paces later by Marion. I brought up the rear.

The darkness faded slowly; pink and golden clouds cut across the light green sky. My back began to warm as the sun rose, and I thought back to Coelho's comments on observing shadows. I watched as the first light created them. They lengthened and then shortened with the influence of the sun. Just like us, I thought. Some influences encourage growth; others dwarf it.

To begin, the edges of some leaves and branches were vague and hard to discriminate. As the light grew stronger, some of the shadows merged; others stood sharply apart. I watched them closely but resorted, as I had the first time, to looking directly at the trees and shrubs. There were two realities to study: one created by sun and shadow, the other a physical reality that left little room for interpretation. I stopped, munched on an apple, and did a breathing exercise before continuing.

It was much later when the sound of hooves broke into my thoughts.

I looked up to see a man leading a donkey whose long ears wobbled as he took each step with caution.

"I envy you your fellow traveller," I said in English. "I have horses back home and sometimes I've felt that they walked here with me."

He stopped and leaned on his walking stick. The donkey turned to the dried grass along the path and began grazing.

"Yes, I always thought I'd do the pilgrimage this way," he said. "I had no idea how to bring a donkey along, but it was dead easy. I bought him back in Santiago."

I looked at him in disbelief. "In Santiago?"

"You got it in one," he announced. "We are walking back to St. Jean-Pied-de-Port." He laughed heartily.

"Any reason for doing that?"

"Just to add a spin to my stories. And I may also walk back to Santiago if George," he gestured to the donkey, "can take it. I think he's fairly old." He rubbed the forelock affectionately. "Well, we need to keep moving. May see you somewhere, who knows?" He laughed again and pulled on the lead shank.

Around one o'clock the heat was unbearable. I stopped, bought a sandwich, and started to look for shade. I soon spotted a man and woman sitting in a grove of trees and shrubs just off the path. They had a bottle of wine and cheese beside them. I walked over. "Buen Camino," I called out. "Mind if I join you in the shade?"

"Hi!" said the man, standing up. "I'm Pascal and my companion," he gestured grandly, "Annik. And what's your name?"

"Patricia," I replied. "D'où venez-vous?" I continued in French. "De la Bretagne," he answered. We talked about the Camino, its meaning, and our experiences over the last two weeks.

"When I get back to France, I will start a group," Pascal said. "We came so unprepared for many aspects of this Camino and we will be so unprepared to pick up our former lives." The conversation continued as we shared the cheese and wine. It wasn't long before they stood up.

"It's been great to meet you," he said as he kissed me on both cheeks.

"I'm sure we'll see you again on this Camino of sorrows!" I waved when they looked back and then leaned against a large tree, munching my apple.

In the near distance, I saw a slight woman striding along with great conviction, her small, neat backpack resting solidly on her back. As she got closer she called out, "I'm stopping for a moment. Could I share your space with you?" Her accent was British and so was her demeanour. She pulled off the pack and dropped it on the dried grass near me. Rummaging around in it, she pulled out a small book. "This is a book of Wordsworth's poems. I've been reading him for several days now." I looked at her in surprise. What a way to start a conversation with a stranger on this scorcher of an afternoon. Must be an English eccentric, I thought to myself, and made up my mind not to get too involved.

"What I like about the poems are his observations on patriotism. Do you know Wordsworth?" she queried. "This is the title of one of his poems where he talks a lot about it. 'I travelled among unknown men.'" She looked at me penetratingly like a teacher assuring I was paying attention. I nodded obediently.

"You see, he was a walker and also travelled a lot outside England. It was when he was away that he recognized his love of his country."

I thought back to my first trip by train to Eastern Canada. I was so excited on the return by the silhouette of the Rockies along the horizon. It was as if I had never seen their beauty before and fell in love with them for the first time. I nodded again, now totally engaged.

"What was it that Camus said?" I asked her. "Something about the value of travel is fear because it opens up the depths of our being?"

"Yes, yes," she concurred. "I remember something like that from a university French class." We smiled at each other.

"It's all about relationships with each other," I added, now confident. "Sometimes we can't even see the connections, but they shape our lives and our feelings. I think of some of it as the images we store in our memory and that flash on the inner screen when they are tapped." There was a silence as I drank from the bottle of water.

She stood up abruptly. "How long have we been talking away?"

"Are you in a rush?" I asked. She shook her head solemnly. "Then let's walk together and keep talking about these great ideas," I suggested.

She looked around slowly. "I think I'd better get going," she said, then picked up her pack and set off at almost a run.

I sat there feeling vaguely rejected. What a strange encounter. I picked up the wrapping paper from the cheese, stuffed it in my pack, and started walking down the ridge.

CHAPTER 11

COMPANIONS

For the last few kilometres into Belorado I walked through a dry, barren world. I could still see the ragged outline of the Sierra de la Demanda, but it brought little relief to the bleak landscape. The town didn't offer much as I entered its outskirts. I could see some modern buildings and the cracked paint and broken windows of a couple of churches; it gave the feeling of being down at the heel. Just beyond the Iglesia Santa Maria there was an elegant three-storey stone building set amongst some trees. The windows on the second and third floors had small wrought-iron balconies; pots of flowers decorated the façade. The door on the ground level was open and I could see a young boy writing at a table.

Suddenly, a short, dark-haired man rushed out, his arms open wide to welcome me. "Your friends are having a beer," he said, smiling. "Please, come and join them." He reached up and grabbed my pack. "My wife Elsa and I are so pleased to have you pilgrims in our new home. Make yourselves at home. Just relax as if you were back in Canada."

I hugged Wendy and Mac as I entered the little bar area.

"Isn't this great?" asked Wendy. "They've shown us the rooms and all the renovations. They're so excited about this place. In fact, they insisted on doing all our laundry! You'd better get yours out so they can put it in. The rooms are lovely, too."

"You'll have to check, Pat, they don't speak a lot of English, but we think we have reserved two." Mac was stretched out on a leather chair, beer in one hand. "David and Marion have gone looking for the local albergue."

I followed Alfredo to the second floor and entered the room he had set aside for me. Its newly painted walls shone. Net curtains moved in the breeze and the duvet was plumped up. He set the pack on a small bench and told me that dinner would be early—and specially prepared—for us. I opened the French doors on the balcony, leaned out, and looked down. I made out a sign, "Verdeancho—Casa Rural," above the main door. Coming along the road were two women carrying bags of groceries, chatting as they walked. They looked up and waved as they passed. I could just make out a word here and there in the staccato Spanish.

"They'll have something to talk about tonight," I thought, certain that Alfredo would fill them in on the Canadians.

I felt a sense of peace and some nostalgia. Somehow, Alfredo and his family did this work together. They had a shared purpose. Even David and Marion had that as they saved their pennies and slept in albergues. Do I have a shared purpose, I wondered.

I turned and headed down the stairs, dirty laundry in hand. Alfredo was standing behind the bar as I came into the pub.

"Tell me, Alfredo, this is the first time I've seen a sign for 'casa rural.' What difference does it make?"

"In a casa rural you have everything—just like being at home. We do laundry, we wake you in the morning, everything. 'Casa' means home. That's us. And our casa dates from the eighteenth century," he replied proudly. "Our renovation was finished, stone by stone, last year." The late afternoon sun streamed through the open windows as we looked and admired the fresh plaster and newly tiled floor.

"Well," said Mac, "I think it's a winner. It has such good vibes. Here come David and Marion. Looks like they've tidied up a bit." He hailed them.

It was much later when I excused myself from the dining room table and left for my room. A feeling of lassitude had taken over and I knew intuitively that I needed to be on my own and get some sleep.

The noise woke me. I was lying on my stomach, my arms wrapped around the pillow. Through half-opened eyes, I could make out the outline of the empty bed beside me, the wallpaper design. What was that noise? Was it coming from Wendy and Mac's room across the hall? I listened intently but didn't hear it. I closed my eyes. Six-thirty would come soon enough. Sleep melted through me.

Then I heard it again. I sat bolt upright, rigid with disbelief.

"It's me!" That sobbing sound was coming from me. I felt my heart beating, slowly and rhythmically. There was no nightmare, no trauma; but sorrow overwhelmed me.

What on earth is wrong with me? This has got to stop. Get your act together, I thought as I turned off my alarm clock. I couldn't let anyone see me like this.

I took several deep breaths determined to regain control. I remembered telling my psychology class that tears were only one of the body's responses to strong emotions. "Never be embarrassed by your tears—or the fact that you can't control them," I had assured them. "It's a normal, acceptable response to strong emotions."

What had provoked such overwhelming emotions? Could I even identify which emotions I felt? I recalled the events of the previous days—the flat, hard meseta land, the heat of the midday, and the simple passionate beauty of the church of St. Eunate. I had cried because of that beauty. Words had failed me entirely and tears had flowed. But that wasn't the reason for this morning's tears.

I crawled out of bed hoping anxiously that it wasn't the flu. Maybe I'd take a couple of Vitamin C.

Alfredo had prepared a hot breakfast and Wendy and Mac were just finishing up. Our host told us his family was still sleeping, but that he enjoyed being up to make our breakfast. His eyes were as red and swollen as mine, I thought to myself. I made a few perfunctory jabs at the omelette and tried to keep the conversation going. Wendy was looking at me closely.

"Sleep well?" she asked. I shrugged, unable to reply.

"It's time to hit the road," declared Mac. "We told David and Marion we'd meet them just before seven." He folded his napkin and I asked Alfredo about settling the bill, including the sandwiches he'd prepared for us.

While Mac took care of that Wendy asked quietly, "Would you like me to walk a ways with you this morning?" I blinked and shook my head.

A short time later, following Mac and Wendy, I headed out of the hotel. We reached the second arrow, gleaming yellow under the street lamp where David and Marion were waiting.

We walked together for a few minutes, Wendy keeping pace with me. The sky was spotted with a few late stars, and other pilgrims cast shadows as they passed us. The silence between Wendy and me was palpable. I glanced over at her just as she said softly, "You know, Pat, I was in tears a couple of days ago. It would start in the morning and then off and on all day."

"I never noticed, Wendy," I said, ashamed that I had been so unaware.

"I tried to cover it as best I could. It seemed so childish to cry without any reason. I hoped that Mac wouldn't notice how long it lasted. He knew, of course, that I was crying that first morning." There was a pause. "I've thought a lot about it since. It seemed to me that all sorts of unresolved tears and sadness were stored in my body. The walking freed them up. So I cried for unknown and forgotten sorrows."

I looked at her profile; she didn't meet my look. My cheeks were wet.

"It means a lot to me that you've talked about it, Wendy," I repressed a sob. "I feel terrible that I didn't even notice." She touched my shoulder.

They began to move away from me, their pace lengthening. Wendy caught up to Mac. I raised my hand to take up her offer of walking together and then dropped it. Whatever caused my tears was in my world; I'd have to handle it myself.

Mac's back was hunched forward under the weight of his backpack; Wendy had added some of her heaviest things. She was looking up at him, as always, as though waiting for him to do I never knew what or to share some hidden secret. Just like me, I thought distractedly; I wanted something on this walk. I tried to quicken my pace and then remembered. Walking too much faster was tiring. I slowed down.

The sun cracked the horizon; the sky turned a sparkling pink. Dust from the rubble of stones and gravel that we walked over filtered the early light. Other pilgrims walked by me, their sticks and staves beating out their rhythm.

My body sank into my familiar pace. Dumb thing to call it, I thought, as a passing pilgrim turned to me and said, "Buen Camino." A pace gets you somewhere; what's this doing for me? Then I reminded myself that we were at kilometre 295—nearly a third of the way. I turned my attention to my walking stick and began counting steps to be in tune with the rhythm. As I did this, the sadness receded. An hour later, in a much lighter frame of mind, I began creating a new rhythm as I usually did by bouncing the walking stick against my thighs. With each step I chanted the body-spirit-heart-mind mantra. For periods of time, I counted in Spanish. The bruised feelings were still lurking in my body, but my spirits lifted.

I had walked alone all morning, seen no one, and passed through empty silent streets in the small towns. Even the sky seemed empty. I longed to be with people, to be in my own home, to stop this endless walk. Tears stayed just below the surface.

I saw a woman looking closely at apples in baskets near the door of a small town market. She was wearing a backpack and there was a scallop shell attached to it. I walked over and asked, "You're doing this pilgrimage, too, aren't you?"

She looked up from the apples she was searching through and smiled. "Yes, I am. You, also?" I heard the French Canadian accent like a leitmotif in her voice. She had dark, penetrating black eyes, olive complexion, and an animated expression.

I had a sudden recollection of a conversation. "I remember meeting you in Los Arcos."

She shrugged her shoulders. "Well, that may be, but I don't remember." We continued side by side, choosing fruit, looking for almonds.

"Where are you heading today?" I asked.

"To Atapuerca. That's about ten or so kilometres farther. And you?"

"Me, too. I'm meeting my friends there for supper and that's where we'll stay the night."

My throat tightened. I felt tears stand in my eyes. The lineup was short and we walked out of the market together. It was midday and overcast, windy and dull looking.

A man walked across the road toward us. "Hélène," he said. "I've found some good bread and salami that'll do us for lunch."

I recognized Geoff before he came up to us. He had that boyish look that some middle-aged American men have. He was slightly bald, lean, and was smiling at Hélène. He looks smitten, I thought. I turned to look at her. Her jaw was set and she wasn't smiling.

I heard my voice from somewhere in my chest, "Today, I could really use some TLC." They both looked surprised, now totally focused on me. "Would you mind if I walk with you for an hour. I'm a really slow walker so you may not want to."

I'm babbling, I thought. What do they care about my pace?

"My friends walk faster than me and that's okay, but today I really need someone to talk with." My voice faded and I looked at them, disconsolate. The desire to cry was strong and I swallowed a gulp.

Hélène spoke first. "Well, sure that's okay. I'm not walking fast today. I have blisters."

"So do I. I've got blisters, too." God, I'm babbling again. "But I just need company and I have always walked slowly."

Geoff grinned at me. "I remember you," he said. "We met in the restaurant a couple of nights ago." I suddenly remembered he had had walking companions.

"What's happened to Franz and Helmut," I asked. "Did they stop—or I guess maybe they're such fast walkers that they've moved past you?"

Geoff nodded and said, "Yes, they've passed me now. So we're walking together for a while." His face glowed with a smile. "Let's make a threesome."

We headed toward the yellow arrow that beckoned from a stone wall. As I walked by I saw how the paint had run. I visualized a Spaniard, brush in hand, slapping on paint. I imagined him as a walker, someone who knew intimately where pilgrims looked for signs and how often we needed them. We walked silently at first, concentrating on walking, on the breeze, and the coolness of the midday.

Geoff adjusted his pace to walk beside me. I felt a surge of gratitude. "You're like a Swiss guide I know. You can change pace," I remarked, delighted.

He gave me a smile. "Yep," he said, "I've had lots of experience walking and I know how to do that. I've walked a lot with my daughters in the US."

"So, tell me, Geoff, where are you from? What do you do? You know, all that stuff."

"I'm a retired navy commander, but I come from Tucson, Arizona."

"Well, you don't sound like you're from the south."

"That's because I'm not! I'm originally from Connecticut. The navy took me all around the world, so my wife and I chose a place to raise our daughters and a southern city like Tucson seemed a good idea at the time." He looked pensive. "But the really interesting person here is Hélène. She's an artist."

"I love the arts. What do you do? Paint? Sculpt?" I'm interrupting again, I thought. Why can't I just have a conversation?

"Well, I was a nurse first. With six kids in Lac St. Jean and believing in education, my mother said to me, 'Find a scholarship so you get educated.' So I did. Nursing was my career until I was fifty and my kids were grown up. Then I said to my husband, to Bernard (she pronounced his name in French), it's my time now. I've helped you with your career; you're successful and I've raised our kids. They're in university. So I became an artist, a painter."

"My mother painted," I interrupted again. "She started at the same age. Did you find it hard to start again?"

"When I was young I had a talent for drawing and when I went back I found the talent was even stronger. That surprised me. But it also gave me confidence."

"What kind of painting do you do?" I asked, avid to know more.

"Are you sure you want to hear about this?" she asked. Geoff and I said "Yes" at the same time.

"My last exhibit was in Montreal. I called it 'le regard du taupe.' Do you know what that means?"

"No," said Geoff.

"It means the gaze of the—what is the word in English?" She looked at me.

"It's a mole," I said.

"So it is a series of paintings, drawings, etc., of how the mole sees the world. Up close, myopic, that's his world. The pieces hang at random throughout the room. I have only one title 'le regard du taupe,' and I let others make sense out of the scenes."

"And do they?" I asked.

"It is so surprising to me, but yes, they do. All unique and different, of course, but they see their world in the taupe-mole's world."

I could imagine the panels as she continued to describe them. As she talked she became more animated.

"My first exhibition was drawings." She looked at us as though gauging how much she could reveal. "It was very simple. You know how you exhale in yoga exercises? Well, I took an immense Japanese writing brush." She spread her arms wide. "Then I placed it on very fine parchment paper, large pieces, maybe three or four feet by two feet. As I exhaled I let the brush slide along the paper. I discovered that I exhale in two stages so the drawings show that clearly. And, besides, each breath is unique; so each drawing was unique. I hung them all—about twenty-five pieces—in an exhibit hall. They were up for a long time. So many people kept coming that the curator just left them up. They were neat," she added lamely. In my mind's eye I could see the fine paper, the black lines each slightly different from the others. The marks of her life and her spirit, I thought.

Geoff looked at her in deep admiration. "Hélène, that's wonderful," he said.

We walked on in silence.

"Why are you on the Camino?" I asked.

"Well," Geoff spoke up, "I retired early from the navy. At forty-five. I've been dabbling in stuff since then. Doing a lot of sailing, travelling, working internationally. I've had a series of contracts. This walk is a sort of gift to myself." He looked out at the horizon. "I wanted to do it as soon as I heard about it a couple of years ago. My daughter is joining me just before Santiago. She'll walk and get a 'credencial,' as the Spanish call it. She's really big on things like that. She likes certificates of achievement. Got a wall papered with them." He laughed shortly. "She's in the middle of a divorce and that's tough."

"And you, Hélène?"

"Well, for me, this is a pilgrimage. I'm a Catholic of the Quiet Revolution, the sixties in Quebec, when we renounced the church in our society. So I am non-practising, but this Camino, this pilgrimage, has taken me by the throat. I had to do it. My mother-in-law, she died two days before my departure. I told Bernard that I would not stay for the funeral. I was going on a pilgrimage and I wouldn't change my plans."

I looked at her in amazement. "You left before the funeral?" Even though the sixties saw huge changes in the Catholic Church in Quebec and the role of women, I couldn't imagine she'd done that.

"Well, no. I left the morning after the funeral. Bernard, he, well, he cried and asked me to stay. He said, 'She is my mother; I need you to be here for me at the funeral.'" She walked a little more slowly, eyes on the ground. "She was not a nice woman," she said after a pause. "I am married now to her son for twenty-eight years. She terrified me when I was first married."

"Tell me, where did you learn English?" I asked.

"There was no English spoken in Lac St. Jean when I was growing up so I watched English television. That's how I learned; I've never taken a class. For a time, I was afraid to say a word at social events. I was so shy." She chuckled. "But my husband wanted me to go with him—so I took my courage in both hands ..."

The silence lengthened. The clouds had disappeared and the midday sun was warm and jolly.

"So, Pat," said Geoff, "what's your take on this marathon?"

I explained my three commonplace goals: my love of the Spanish language, Gothic architecture, and a visit to a new part of Spain. For a moment, I weighed whether to tell them of the changes in my goals. "And lately, I have recognized that the real goal for me is spiritual."

Geoff coughed slightly. Hélène turned to me and said, "What does that word mean to you?"

"It means the bliss of living each moment. It means the sense of integration between the body, soul, mind, and heart. It means walking in this stable, knowable, agreed-upon world and being able to walk in those other worlds—worlds that were always there, but we never visited."

"What worlds are those?"

"Well, that's a much longer conversation, of course. Let's stop for lunch and talk about them," I suggested.

We stretched out on the grass. We were in the shade of a tree facing a magnificent valley, lush with trees and grass. In the distance, grey-blue mountains were linked along the horizon. We put our lunch buys together and shared a tin of sardines.

I told them about Indio, about working with my horses. "The gift for us as humans is their unmediated emotions. The communication with animals has a different dimension. They don't reason, analyze, or judge—none of that. They just are. That's their gift to us. I believe this is like an untapped source of being. If you think of people who train animals, whose lives have been transformed by them, you recognize a unique quality: a sort of calm, a different energy."

"That's like carrying a baby," said Hélène. "You both can sense each other's responses without words." Geoff cut another slice of bread.

"That image is so powerful, Hélène," I said. "The world they open for us—if we let them—is deep within us. For me, it seems to be another reality, deeper, seamless, a layer of our being that goes beyond logic and formal study. It is like the Tao—it can be embraced but not defined."

That was the first of many conversations I knew I would live in as I walked my Camino and far beyond it.

—⚬⚬⚬—

CHAPTER 12

SURVIVORS

W e arrived in Atapuerca in late afternoon. Hélène and Geoff were staying in albergues so they left in search of the best one. I wandered slowly along the street into town savouring the afternoon. It wasn't long before Wendy and Mac hailed me from in front of a small hotel. They were with David and Marion seated around a table that had empty bottles and dishes with the remains of tapas.

"This is becoming an everyday event," I said, gesturing to the remains on the table.

David beckoned to the waiter. "A *cerveza* for the lady," he announced.

"I'm impressed, Davy boy," I said sarcastically. "Your vocabulary is expanding!" I poured the beer as the others laughed.

"Looks like your day was a good one, Pat!" Wendy said. "You're really attacking that beer."

"It's been wonderful. I walked with two fascinating people all afternoon. One was *canadienne* from Montreal and the other—"

"So did we," interrupted David, looking at Mac with great admiration. He turned back to me, "You'll have to tell us more!"

I looked at him, feeling prickles of irritation under my scalp. He had a natural gift for getting under my skin. Marion sat beside him, expressionless.

"I have more important things to do, David," I snapped, the irritation rough in my voice. I picked up my glass of beer and said, "Cheers!"

There was a burst of nervous laughter. Mac turned, grinned at me, and said, "Thought you were going to throw that beer, Pat! Kinda glad you didn't."

"So am I, Pat," said David, laughing. "Figured I might be the target." He laughed again, his eyes fixed on me. Wendy and Mac joined in. I smiled, still feeling grim.

Around seven o'clock, we found a small restaurant that had opened early to cater to pilgrims. As we walked in, I looked around the room. It was alive with the sights and sounds of pilgrims talking, laughing, calling out to each other. My eyes were drawn irresistibly to a small table against the wall. It was slightly to one side, away from the noisy talk, bustling waiters, and the scuffle of chairs. Its position defined a distance that was not solely physical. Its inhabitants were sitting opposite each other, staring off into space. Her hand was stretched out toward him; they seemed in contact although there was not the slightest touch. They sat in stark contrast with the activity of the restaurant. A bubble of silence and stillness embraced them. I realized I was staring and turned to Wendy.

"Did you notice those pilgrims sitting over there?" I nodded in their direction, speaking softly so no one could hear us. "What do you make of it?"

Her eyes penetrated mine. "Did you feel like talking this morning? Didn't a nod seem like an effort?" she asked. "There were times," she continued, "for me, when talk, sound was more than I could bear." She paused. "You know, I don't think what you and I have experienced is the exception. Others have got to feel the sadness, the tears, and the pain, too. It's a part of walking the Camino. We now see with new eyes. Our fellow travellers come from all periods of time—the past, the present—and the many worlds of the Camino."

I nodded. Then, deep inside me, I relived my flash of irritation with David. In some way, that anger and the sadness I had been feeling came from the same source.

The waiter arrived to tell us about the menu, which included fresh halibut imported from the north Atlantic. When it arrived it surpassed all expectations.

"This is the best meal we've had since we started the Camino," I said to the waiter in Spanish. He smiled blandly and replied, "Everyone says the same thing."

I turned to the others and announced, "The other great thing is that this wine is perfect with it."

"Delusions!" snorted Mac. "Two glasses ago, this wine was for all intents and purposes undrinkable. Don't underestimate the power of denial."

"Something else, folks. Our Camino is progressing. We are getting stronger—or at least I think we are—and each of our paces is carrying us along smoothly." I looked around the table.

There was a short silence.

"Here's to our commitment to do this walk together." I raised my glass and clinked with theirs. "Our different paces are a reminder of how each of us is unique. Our pace is our identity. So we start together in the morning and we have dinner in the evening—as a minimum. Each day is ours to be walked as we see it."

We talked about our commitment to the Camino, to our dreams of finishing it without taking transportation.

"Tomorrow we'll be in Burgos," I reminded them. "Remember when we talked about goals that first night in St. Jean-Pied-de-Port?" I looked at Wendy and Mac. "You don't know, David and Marion, but one of my major Camino goals is to see the cathedral of Burgos. I can't wait. It's one of Europe's great cathedrals."

"It's close, too. Not much of a walk," said Wendy. "About eight, maybe ten kilometres. We can do that quickly, see the cathedral, and be ready to leave the next morning. One day should do it."

I squirmed; my resistance grew as she talked. "Why don't we wait and see how the afternoon goes? In fact, why don't the five of us just meander into Burgos together? We don't have far to go so we don't have to make record time. Then we could spend the night in Burgos, see the cathedral again in the early morning light. Do all sorts of odds and ends, like Internet, laundry in the afternoon." My voice dwindled off as I looked at the unresponsive faces in front of me. "Well, let's think about it. It could be a good change for us," I said stoutly. We paid the waiter and walked out into a star-studded night.

"It's an evening made for a small glass of cognac," said Mac. David and Marion gave us a hug and headed for the albergue. We walked in silence to a nearby outdoor bar and found a table.

"It's not a bad idea, Pat. For such a short distance we could walk together; maybe even start a little later like eight or eight-thirty," Wendy mused. She turned to Mac. "Let's do it, Mac!" He smiled and nodded.

I watched pilgrims passing by in front of us. "Yeah, why not?" I lifted my glass. "Salud!"

· · ·

I heard the knock on my door around six-fifteen the next morning. "¿Sí?" I called out.

"C'est moi, Patricia." I heard Hélène's voice. I opened the door and gave her a hug.

"You're going already?" I asked in French, looking at the pack on her back.

"Yes, Geoff has already left. He headed off with Sebastian. You remember him? He showed up at the albergue late last night." I nodded. "They decided to head off before sunrise. He said to say goodbye to you and promised to meet up again. Me, I'm going off the Camino to the Monastère de St. Francis near here. I heard last night that the priest there is exceptional. I want to talk to him about my faith—or lack of it. I cannot believe and, yet, I think I do believe in something. So, us, too, we say goodbye. You okay today? You will be fine." We hugged.

I would miss her, but I knew in my heart of hearts that we would walk and talk together again. Yesterday we had talked about the serendipity of meeting each other and how we should trust chance and good fortune to guide our lives.

It was a little before seven when the two couples arrived on the piazza where I was finishing my second coffee.

"You're early—and alone," said Marion, looking around.

"Yes, Hélène came to say goodbye before leaving at six-fifteen this morning. Geoff had already headed out." I lifted my coffee cup. "So grab a coffee and let's go see that cathedral."

We began walking, Mac and David a few steps ahead, Marion, Wendy, and I just behind them. The pace was relaxed and slower than usual.

"I didn't notice last night that you were limping, Pat. What's up?" asked Wendy.

"Nothing that an easy day won't fix," I replied. "My knee started to get sore so I used my knee brace a bit yesterday. It feels a lot better today. And it's lucky today is a short walk." I pulled out my guidebook. "It says to ignore the Camino signs and follow this path along the Río Arlanzón to the city centre." We could make out the buildings of the industrial area and the outline of Burgos on the west.

We were soon following the arrows, which guided us to the N120. Cars and trucks roared past us. At one point, David grabbed his straw hat just before it flew onto the highway. He shouted over the noise, "How do we get over there?" He gestured wildly to the dirt path across from us. There was no foot crossing marked on the highway. We perched precariously on the guardrail before making a wild dash across.

"Go for it," Mac shouted. I ran, the pack bouncing wildly on my back.

"That's as close to kamikaze as I ever want to get," said David, his facing shining with sweat.

We continued along the dirt path over to the tree-lined boulevard, where we could make out other bridges and green areas. We could now see the startling white masonry of the cathedral on our right and the castle on the hill just behind it. I quickened my pace and walked up to Mac and David.

"Looks as though you're racing, Pat," said Mac. "A bit anxious to get there?"

"I've wanted to see this cathedral for ages," I replied. "They've redone the façade, getting rid of centuries of black stain. Even from this distance you can see how beautiful the spires are and the flying buttresses. I can hardly wait to see the stained glass windows." My voice sounded high pitched.

"Whoa," said David. "You're talking awfully fast." I turned to him, a quick retort on my tongue, and then remembered. I hesitated. "No cathedral has ever inspired me like that," he laughed. "In fact, I can't think of anything that's made me walk or talk faster."

"Well, David, my heartfelt wish is that you do find something one day." I tried to laugh but knew how much I meant it.

We walked more quickly until we came to a beautiful bridge called Puente de San Pablo, which guarded the statue of El Cid.

"Who's this noble man?" Marion queried

"That's El Cid, one of Spain's great heroes. In university we studied a French author, Corneille, who wrote a play about him that is now a classic. El Cid was a soldier and a man of letters."

I paused for a moment. "Did you know that one of the biggest influences on building this cathedral was people just like us? Pilgrims who brought stories of the cathedrals of Paris and Île-de-France to Spain? And that was back in the twelfth and thirteenth centuries. They brought along stories of stained glass, statues—you name it."

The cathedral sat in the centre of Burgos surrounded by traffic and noise. Its soaring beauty silenced us. The fine fretwork on the spires, the rose window, and the simplicity and complexity of its bas-reliefs were awe-inspiring.

"I know it's early," said Wendy, "but let's find accommodation. Then we can just visit it without time concerns."

David pulled out his accommodation guide. "There's a sort of hotel-pension in Burgos that is no more expensive than an albergue. We could all stay in the same place again. It's not far from here."

He set off, book in hand. We were soon in front of a monstrous two-storey building, its front grey and weathered, and its roof in need of repairs. I felt doubt surge in me. I had stayed in identical places when I had hitchhiked across Europe. I couldn't imagine this being a good place to stay. A large woman in a drab dress with a soiled apron covering it opened the door. She squinted at us suspiciously.

"You want rooms?" she queried in Spanish.

"Sí, three rooms. Could we see them?" I replied. She nodded and opened the door wider so that we could enter. She led us up a flight of stairs to the second floor. I was overwhelmed by the odour of stale air, by the greyness of the bed linen. I picked up a towel in the bathroom. It was threadbare, the design long since washed out. My throat convulsed and the desire to vomit hit me. I opened a French window and leaned out. Mac came up to me quickly. "Are you okay, Pat?" he asked with concern.

"No, Mac," I replied. "I can't stomach this place—literally. It reminds me of all those hostels I stayed in when I was hitchhiking. I've got to stay somewhere else." I looked down at my boots on the threads of a rug that had seen better days. "I'll wait outside for you."

I practically ran back down the stairs to the door. I could see a small bar across the street. I went over, ordered a beer, and sat down. When the waiter came with my beer, I asked, "Is there another hotel near here?" He gave me the name of a hotel that he assured me was close, clean, and modern.

When Wendy and Mac joined me, I said casually, "Let's go over to Hôtel El Norte y Londres." We walked down a side street and found a modest little hotel with a neon sign where I rented a tiny, clean room.

"I'd say this is too expensive, Pat. Stay with us." David threw me a disapproving glance.

I shrugged and set down my pack. "The cathedral is within a stone's throw," I said. "Time to go see it."

We walked into the cathedral as the late afternoon sun shone through the rose window. Its patterns covered the stone floor, transforming it into a magic carpet of light and colour. I felt each colour individually and saw it so clearly against the alabaster stone. The air was golden, streaming around us. Sitting in a pew near the altar I felt there was nothing to say. What could anyone add? The doors, the spires, the air-filled stairwells—everything had such integrity. There was no detail that was not essential to the whole. The authenticity of the whole gave meaning and purpose at every vantage point.

• ◆ •

The door was marked "Trust" and it swung open wide. I went though it doing backward somersaults in a bright green body suit. The earth's crust had split open and ribbons of molten gold were flowing below me. With an expansive leap I left that landscape and found myself doing handsprings between mounds of burnished copper. My heart expanded with joy, flowers burst into blossom, and grew up to the sky. Birds flew alongside me in the air. When I awoke, I saw joy around me and felt it in the air I was breathing.

At breakfast I told them my dream to gales of laughter. Suddenly, Marion looked up from her coffee and said, "We have something to tell you." David looked at her askance. "Don't say anything, David. I just made up my own mind." She looked Mac, Wendy, and me in the eye and announced solemnly, "Today is our third anniversary! We weren't going to tell you, but this morning, well … "

"Really?" said Wendy. "Let's celebrate! We'll get a bottle of champagne!" She threw her arms around Marion, who was flushed and teary eyed. David sat back, arms crossed.

"Much ado about nothing," he said, smiling. "What's all the fuss?"

"Honestly, David …" Marion began and then stopped. For a moment, they sat speechless, looking at each other, love written on their faces.

"Sort of renews your faith in humanity, doesn't it?" said Mac.

We paid the bill and headed off to an Internet terminal nearby. On the way, we passed one of Burgos's many clothing shops. In the window was a brilliant blue t-shirt with a picture of the Camino and a pilgrim on it.

"Wendy," I called out. "Just look at this. That's one of my favourite colours and the picture could be us."

She looked at my yellow t-shirt, which was grey and pilled.

"You could use a replacement, Pat, maybe even two of them. You really cut it close to the wire." We had each weighed everything as part of packing light. I returned from the shop wearing the new t-shirt and threw out my old one as we passed a garbage can.

It was still dark the next morning when I knocked on Wendy and Mac's door. There was no sound or movement. I headed off to find the albergue where David and Marion were staying. As I came in I saw Wendy and Mac standing near a bunk bed where David and Marion sat, holding hands. The mood was glum.

Marion looked up at me. "David simply can't go any farther, Pat. I'm taking him to a hospital. His feet ..." She gestured to the mass of bandages and blue-black skin. "I'm just a nurse. He needs more medical help than I can give him." She looked anxiously at him, but he didn't meet her eye.

"We will see you again. We've made plans with Wendy and Mac to catch up with you after we see a doctor. "

I smiled at them. "Well, that's Mac's specialty. We always know where we'll be." We laughed, while Mac looked awkward.

It was later than usual when we started walking. "On the road again, I just gotta get on the road again," I started singing. Wendy and Mac joined me and we strode along in rhythm with the music.

We began talking about David's medical problems, others with hip, knee, back problems. Some pilgrims were suffering from simply being too tired or bored or a lack of commitment. It was a constant topic of conversation in the evenings. We were survivors and we felt nervous. Who would be next? We exchanged gossip about those we'd walked with, recalled the topics of conversation.

"Do you remember Sosus, Pat, the guy from Granada?" Mac asked. I nodded.

"Well, he told us this morning that he has decided to stop."

Wendy chimed in. "He said that he started out fit and believed he'd get fitter, but it just wasn't what happened. He's been having problems with his hip and then he got blisters." She paused. "He said that all the hope in the world wasn't enough to keep him going."

We walked on in silence. Sosus was a lot younger than we were. And as a Catholic his commitment to finish the Camino had been strong.

"Let's not talk about that," said Wendy. "We'll just keep on walking and we won't think about problems. We'll keep the faith." She smiled at us, but neither Mac nor I said anything.

"Just to change the topic, Pat, how old is Hélène?" Mac suddenly asked. He loved the details: age, marital status, job, education.

"I have absolutely no idea, Mac. That's a question I'd never ask—unless the person was dead!"

Wendy burst out laughing. "He's writing this stuff in his diary every night," she confided. "All the details. Just like when we got married. He kept track of each time we made love—and gave it a grade. I told him he had to stop—unless he entered my grading, too. He didn't want that much detail." Mac looked embarrassed. She put her arm around him and gave him a hug.

"Well, at least you can still blush, Mac. My mother would say you have a streak of decency left in you." I winked at him.

He turned to Wendy. "Our marriage is a triumph of hope and experience," he said, and kissed her on the cheek. And it shows, I thought.

Mac paused for a moment, got up off the grass, and offered his hand to Wendy. They kissed; we swung our packs up and left. An hour later, we arrived in front of a small coffee shop.

"¿Café con leche?" Mac asked. We stopped, had our coffee, and then picked up our walking pace. Soon Wendy and Mac were well ahead of me.

I walked on, recollecting our recent conversations, moments of silence, and laughter. Our world was defined more and more as we spent time together and shared purpose and meaning.

That night we walked into the little town of Castrojeriz and rented rooms in a large hotel overlooking the valley and the town. Early in the evening, in the warmth of the sun, I hung out my washing in the windows of my room. The smell of wet clothing, the heat, and the sound of Spaniards talking below me filled me with contentment. I went down the stairs to the patio, ordered a beer, and began writing in my diary. I was still fascinated by my ongoing experiences with the shadows and how meaning could be constructed without consciously setting out to do it. I wrote for a couple of pages, but the desire wasn't there.

"Time to give it a break," I said out loud. I turned my attention to another table where four men were playing a card game. The silence was intense, their eyes focused on the cards. One man slapped a card down on the table. He looked at the others expectantly. The second man placed his card with exaggerated care on top of it. They all laughed and the loud excited voices filled the area. Leaning forward, the first man slapped the other's shoulder. They gestured, laughed.

"Aren't they intense?" said Mac. "I love watching them. Tell me what's going on."

"The second guy just won and now they're replaying the game," I replied. "Those black eyes and the incredible music of their language—it's so engaging. I wish I spoke more Spanish."

We sat watching them as the heat, and the game, lingered on into the evening.

CHAPTER 13

PAIN AND COMFORT

I t was early and still very dark when I dressed hurriedly, packed, and opened my door. Mac and Wendy were waiting. We crossed the courtyard in silence, looking for the yellow arrows.

"Over here," called Wendy softly. "I've found an arrow."

In the dark we saw two lights bobbing up and down. Jorge and his wife Hortensia, from Chicago, were walking just ahead of us wearing their night lights. We greeted each other in whispers.

"The valley is full of fog," said Jorge. "But it won't stop us." The five of us fell into rhythm. As we passed under a lone street light I suddenly found myself lying flat on the cement sidewalk. I heard the groan as my backpack hit the back of my head and my chin and nose slammed into the cement.

"God, Pat, what's happened?"

"Don't move her. She may be hurt."

I tried to stand, to regain my balance, but was unable to find my feet. I put my hand on my jaw and moved it. Thank God, it wasn't broken. Shock spread through my body.

I felt strong arms helping me up, taking off my backpack. "What on earth happened to you? One moment we were walking and the next you were on the ground?" Jorge's voice was anxious and his accent suddenly thick.

"You're okay," said Wendy. "There's nothing wrong. Let's start walking."

I stared at her. Her voice was strong and authoritative. Pain rippled through my body.

"See. She's okay," she repeated. "Her knee isn't even bleeding. Let's go."

"Perhaps you'd like to sit down," said Mac, helping me over to a park bench. I sat down, my head in my hands. I could feel my chin swelling. The world swirled around me.

"How the hell did that happen?" I asked.

"You're okay," said Wendy again. "Let's start walking."

"But the pain is qu-qu-ite—" I stammered.

"Your knee isn't bleeding," she said once more. I could see her face now. It was white, her eyes looked black.

"You know, Pat," said Mac, ignoring Wendy's comments, "maybe you should take a bus. You're likely in shock. It would be better not to walk. How are you feeling? What do you think?"

I listened to the tone of his voice. I marvelled at how quickly he took charge of the situation in this little Spanish town at seven in the morning. Must be natural, I thought irrelevantly.

As I sat there waiting for the pain to subside, I conjured up being in the bus. I could just imagine myself dozing in the warmth at the back of a Greyhound bus. My pack was on the seat beside me, the sunrise lighting the road and the hills. I wanted nothing more than to be transported. I didn't want to walk. But as I sat there, a voice deep inside me asked, "So what has your chin got to do with your feet? With how you walk?" And I knew the answer. Holding onto my stick, I got shakily to my feet.

"Nope, I'm walking. Let's go." We started off again.

Soon the natural pace took over. Jorge and Hortensia moved out, quickly recouping lost time. Mac and Wendy followed a few steps behind. I put my head down and focused on my rhythm. The fog was so thick I could barely make out the trees. The stones under my feet were rough and scattered.

How the hell did I fall like that? I replayed the scene. I had no recollection of falling. It was as though I had been felled. My knee had touched the sidewalk but wasn't bruised, only scraped. The sun pierced the fog and the sunrise filled the sky. I began to breathe more deeply. The path suddenly turned steep. I leaned on my walking stick for balance with each step.

What happened next was as unexpected as the fall in Castrojeriz. A warmth settled across my shoulders and I was suddenly surrounded by love and compassion. I felt my father's presence, his strength flow through me. His arm was warm and heavy on my shoulders. He was walking on my left, his head bowed. I tried to make eye contact with him, but his eyes were averted. His presence lay so deep within me that my breathing became a part of it. It was as though the depth of his love and compassion defined me. His compassion was as real as the stones on the path where I walked.

We walked up the steep ridge; his arm now supported me. My eyes overflowed. He was my father, whose love and care was unconditional. He had come now because I needed to understand that truth. Without words, these feelings, this knowledge filled the space in which I lived and walked.

Just as suddenly his presence evaporated. I was alone on the trail near the top of the ridge. The sun beat down on my back. I was left with the certainty that he loved me unconditionally, that he had compassion for my suffering.

At the top of the rise, Hortensia looked at me. "You need an ice pack. Have you got one?" I started to laugh, my voice sounded strangely wobbly.

"Yes, back in Calgary."

She reached into her pack and pulled out a small pack of synthetic ice and rubbed it between her hands. "Then take mine!"

I hugged her. She lent me a dark headscarf. "We'll make you a sling to hold the ice up against your chin," she said as she wrapped the soft silk against my face. It felt warm and comforting. The ice took my mind off the swelling.

"Let's get going," said Jorge. And together we turned and continued walking. The vivid image of my father had disappeared, but not the feeling of being embraced. From this point on, I promised myself, no more doubts. I'll walk all of the Camino. The knowledge was certain and deep inside me.

A short while later, I was walking slightly behind Wendy and Mac. "My father walked with me today," I said, my voice taut and thin. The horizon grew fuzzy. I looked down quickly and heard Mac say, "That must have been quite an experience." I just nodded.

•   •   •

We had agreed to meet David and Marion at a small albergue built on the ruins of a medieval hospital. The albergue had a unique reputation—beds had white sheets, waiters served beer. It took me the remainder of the afternoon to make it there. I was walking alone, well behind the others, when I saw a patch of green against the cinnamon earth. Boadilla! The path leading to the entrance was made of blocks of stone, with deeply worn grooves. The grass was rich in contrast to the plain soil tilled into lumps. It resembled the Alhambra—white stones, the presence of water, the oasis in a dry land.

As I walked into town a woman's voice called out in Spanish, "¡Patricia, qué bueno!" I turned to see Rosita, a *madrileña*, running toward me. She threw her arms around me and kissed me on both cheeks then started back with a look of horror on her face. "What has happened to your face? Good heavens! What a terrible injury! Have you seen a doctor? When did it happen?"

I was stumbling with my answers in Spanish. "Nada, nada, Rosita. I fell this morning and hit my chin. That's all. No, I don't want to go to a doctor. Believe me, it will look worse in a couple of days."

Her excitement didn't change. "But look at you, mi amiga, you are so thin. You have changed so much and had a terrible injury, too."

I laughed and hugged her. "Well, if this walk doesn't help me lose weight nothing will! I'm glad to hear I've changed form—and really, don't worry about the injury. I am very lucky. Nothing is broken. It was just a fall."

"Well," said a man's voice slowly but in Spanish, "that's how it all began. With a fall from grace." I turned to see an older, tall, slender man pushing a bike. His beret was sitting jauntily on his head.

"Hola, Norbert," said Rosita. "Patricia, this is my friend. He also lives in Canada. He is a professor there."

He took my hand and kissed it with an exaggerated movement. "Mis amigas," he said and gestured to the bike with a flourish. "This is my noble steed Rocinante. Like me, she is old and decrepit. She has seen better days but her loyalty is unquestioned."

We began to laugh with him. He actually did look a little like Don Quixote.

"Will you come and have a drink with me?" he offered. We pulled up chairs in the shade and opened cans of beer. The cool liquid was like ambrosia. I looked at the pilgrims lounging in the shade, and heard the laughter and the murmur of voices.

"So tell me, Norbert, how is it you are here on the Camino?"

"It's like this," he said. "I was an undergraduate in Vienna—I am from Vienna. One day I happened to overhear some Spanish students talking. I fell in love with the language just like that." He snapped his fingers. "So that was how I began my long quest to court this language and make it my own. I love it so much." He spoke slowly, eloquently; his Austrian accent added some piquancy. "I am walking the Camino to find answers for my retirement. And you, Patricia, why are you on a pilgrimage?"

"Come over and meet my two Canadian friends. We'll tell you the whole story of our decision to walk the Camino." We walked over to where Wendy and Mac were having a beer and sat down with them. The courtyard was strikingly beautiful. Large blocks of stone from Roman times were arranged throughout. Beds of flowers flourished in the shade of a long stone wall that wrapped itself around the area. In the centre was a statue of two pilgrims. The iron had rusted, but this only enhanced the story: a tall angular pilgrim leaning heavily on his staff and another one seated, one shoe off, his head turned down, doctoring his feet. Beside the statue was a pool. Such a luxury in this heat and dryness. Laundry hung from a clothesline, pilgrims lolled on the grass, and the sun touched everyone.

We sat on the stones in a shady part of the patio surrounded by conversations in Spanish and English. The tones and the rhythms blended soothingly in the heat of the afternoon. I leaned back against a large rock and let my mind go over the day's events. I recalled the fog and the filtered light of the street lamp where I had fallen. I touched my jaw gingerly for the hundredth time just to make sure the joint still worked. It was sore and moved slowly, but it still moved. It will never make sense to me, I thought, as I replayed the early morning scene. My throat constricted as I felt my father's presence.

"How are you enjoying your beer?" asked a familiar voice. I turned to find myself face to face with David. He gave me a hug, took me by the shoulders, and stood back to make eye contact.

"My God," he squawked in alarm. "What did you do to your face? To your neck? I leave you for a couple days and look what you've done to yourself!" Wendy and Mac started to laugh and Marion joined in. We exchanged hugs.

What he said was true. Earlier in the afternoon, when I had taken off the ice pack I'd seen my face in a mirror. It was grotesque. My chin was black and blue, scratched and swollen. The colours continued down my neck into my collar.

"How goes it, David?" Mac asked.

"Good, good," he replied, avoiding his wife's eyes. "We'll make 'er."

There was a pause in the conversation. "So, Pat," he turned to me. "How are your feet?"

"Just enough pain to remind me that I'm walking on them," I said light-heartedly. "And yours?"

Marion spoke up quickly. "He's in pain again, Pat. It will take longer than two days to heal his blisters." She gestured and I looked down. David's feet were still covered in blisters and in some places the swelling was visible through the sandal straps.

"Good heavens, David," Mac exclaimed. "Did you see a doctor? You ought to go again."

Rosita turned to me and said in Spanish, "Yes, before he loses some toes."

"It's not bad, mate," said David. "You know that Sosus has dropped out because of his knees? And I hear that Annette also is having troubles. Who knows how many others?" There was a moment's silence.

"Has anyone seen Jorge and Hortensia? You know the professor from Chicago and his Mexican wife? The ones we started with this morning?" asked Wendy.

"The last time I saw them they were getting into a bus. That was not long after she gave me the ice pack," I recalled.

"Let's have another beer," said Mac. Just then another couple walked over to us.

"Here come Michael and Yolanda, from Krakow. We just met them," said Wendy.

The courtyard was a haven, encompassed by the stone wall, embracing the gifts of the water and the sculpture and protected from the direct sun by the tall shrubs and trees. In the safety of its perimeter we moved back and forth, meeting one another. When evening came, the light was fine and discreet, touching the statues, the stones, and the faces turned toward the sunset. Peace settled into our little community. At seven-thirty we went over to the small, insignificant-looking church for evening mass. The sermon that night was dedicated to the pilgrims. The priest looked out over his very small crowd, made the sign of the cross, and blessed us. We made our way slowly back to the albergue.

The next morning I walked into the bathroom, holding the door open for Norbert behind me. Faces, backs, the smells of shampoo, soap, and bodies assaulted me. I'll never get used to communal bath areas, I thought. Wendy's right. I am just too middle class.

I found a free shower stall and luxuriated in the hot water, the soap on my body. I stayed for what seemed an eternity, my hands on the wall, leaning into the stream of water. As I went back to my bunk I passed the open door of the dining room. The smell of coffee and toast wafted out. I looked inside and saw pilgrims being served a prepared breakfast—something I hadn't seen since starting the walk—a rare treat! Some were already leaving, others talking softly.

The sky was inky black as we headed off toward the hills we'd seen
the evening before. Our silence was comfortable. The fog was lighter
than yesterday's. It softened the light from the street lamp and the lines
of buildings. We could see shapes disappearing in its density while others
materialized in front of us. As we went along peering into the darkness
looking for the familiar yellow arrow, we saw the Aussies. David walked
with a pronounced limp.

"Hey, you pilgrims," Mac whispered. "Are you heading west to
Santiago?" They turned and greeted us, teeth showing in the dark. Our
steps fell in unison. In front of us and behind us we could hear the sound
of boots on the rough-hewn Roman road. We walked as had thousands
before us on those stones.

"They built to last," whispered David. "Some engineers, those guys."

The arrows led us to the trail that turned and followed the banks of
the Canal de Castilla. The fog was heavier along the canal; the light had
an eerie ominous glow. The morning was windless, yet there was the
impression of people moving alongside of us. They appeared and then
disappeared as the fog thickened or thinned for no apparent reason. I could
hear David and Mac laughing ahead of me and then Wendy and Marion
disappeared into the fog at the next bend.

I wondered if I'd ever get used to the moment when they pulled away
from me and I began walking alone.

CHAPTER 14

A WORLD OF
DIFFERENCE

T he fog was heavier yesterday morning, and today the land had
changed. It was flat and stark according to the map Mac consulted
that morning. Sometimes I could make out the stubble at the edge
of the harvested fields from the paved footpath I was following. I swung
my walking stick and caught the end of it in my left hand. I plodded along
tapping out the rhythm, chanting my mantra. Sweat ran down my back,
and my feet swelled and ached.

With no effort—in fact, in spite of myself—yesterday's events came
back. I viewed them at arm's length, feeling nothing, seeing or hearing
snippets as though from an expurgated version. The fall echoed in my
body; the weight of the pack reminded me how it had hit the back of my
head. It didn't happen to me, not really, I comforted myself.

The sunrise, hot red and yellow, transformed the last of the fog and
exposed the flat, dry land. As the heat penetrated, I took off the scarf,
unzipped my jacket, and forced my thoughts away from yesterday's events.
Yet, the image of my father stayed with me, loving and compassionate.

Sprawling and modern, Frómista was without interest except for the
songbirds on the Río Ucieza. Their cheerful, bright colours stood out
against the white walls. The pervasive silence was interrupted from time

to time by the sound of my boots on the gravel and the hollow echo as I crossed the arched stone bridges.

By contrast, the town of Villalcázar de Sirga welcomed me as I walked up to the massive Romanesque-Gothic church of Santa Maria la Blanca at the entrance into the town. The church door was open and I stepped into the cool darkness with great relief. There was statue of the Virgen Blanca with a squat, headless baby Jesus. I stood for a while looking at this strange sight. The glaring sun shone through the stained glass, mottling the statue and the stone floor. I pulled the door shut and headed toward a small bar on the main street.

"Where are all the pilgrims today?" I grumbled, ordering a beer. The bartender stared at me, expressionless.

"This is a lonely, brutal walk," I complained to the top of his head as he bent to pour my glass.

He shrugged and replied, "Cinco euros, por favor." The beer was cold and sharp, a welcome change.

At the end of the afternoon I arrived in Carrión de los Condes where Wendy and Mac had booked us rooms in a hotel near the centre.

"I salute your good taste," I announced as I sat down at the table with them. "Even the idea of a bed and some privacy is good."

Wendy stood up. "I'm heading in for a shower. David and Marion will come over from the refugio later and we'll eat together." I watched her as she walked to the hotel. There was a leftover coolness since the fall. I shrugged. It would work itself out, I thought—or it wouldn't.

Mac and I sat on a short stone wall at the edge of the village, without talking. The sun was setting just above the line of hills; the silence was companionable as we sipped on our beers. The harsh light of sunset made shadows on the tilled fields. A flock of sheep was spread out along the ridge and just behind it walked a shepherd with his dogs, responding to his every gesture.

"Do you remember those little handouts they gave us in Sunday school, Mac?" I asked. "This looks like it was the set for those pictures."

We headed back to our hotel, which was tucked away near the main street. The barman greeted us with a grunt. Even my Spanish had no charm over him.

"Not his day, I guess," Mac said, raising his glass in a toast.

It was near midnight when I got back to my room. The light over the sink was dim, but I could make out the bruises. At supper, Marion had explained that my earaches were from the bruising I got when I fell. I had a flashback of the jolt, and my jaw slamming back.

The next morning, I observed my bruised face in the mirror, filling the room. I stood up and leaned against the bed. Anxiety welled up in my chest. Again, I felt the fall, the impact of the pack, and the unforgiving cement sidewalk. Don't dwell on it, I reprimanded myself.

The heat was building by the time we left the hotel. The clouds were outlined in ghostly white and moving slowly against the black sky. The clatter of our boots on the cobblestone broke the silence. Dark forms lurked in the shadows along the street. A sense of foreboding lingered, perhaps from the violent history of Carrión de los Condes. It was here that the daughters of El Cid were beaten by their bridegrooms, the Counts. As a father, El Cid took revenge. He murdered the men and buried them here in the Monasterio. And so that no one would ever forget he named the town Carrión de los Condes, "the rotting carcasses of the Counts." I shivered and picked up my pace. Soon Wendy and I were in step.

"You did an undergraduate degree in literature, too, didn't you, Wendy?" I asked. She looked over her shoulder at me and nodded.

"Do you remember the play about El Cid? This is the place where it all happened. Maybe that's why it seems so ominous this morning." I gestured to the sweep of dun-brown landscape and the distant silhouette of the town we were walking toward.

"Remember, the play was about the importance of honour. El Cid's dilemma was to choose between honour and love. Honour was most important. If you sacrificed your honour, you had nothing and you were nothing."

Wendy smiled. "I used to wonder who chose the texts for eighteen-year-old Western Canadian students—well, for kids generally. I couldn't even spell the word 'honour.'" We walked on in silence.

"Just the same, the code in my family was if you gave your word you never broke it. It was a question of honour. It was grueling being brought up under such a code," I said. I remembered how my mother had told no one in her family about my divorce. Three years after it was over, I surprised my aunt when I told her I was on my own. When I asked she said that no one knew anything about it. The classics aren't esoteric, I thought to myself. They identify the eternal themes and give us the space to think them through and to see how they play themselves out in our lives. We walked on in silence in the growing heat of the morning.

"So, do you want to stop in Calzadilla de la Cueza?" Mac took off his sunglasses and looked at each of us. We were seated in the meagre shade of a church wall, the air shimmering in front of us. "We could go on to Sahagún. It's over forty kilometres, but …" He paused. "I know it's long but remember that we did thirty-two clicks on day one and survived." No one spoke.

"We could stop at the refugio in Calzadilla," Wendy's voice was pointed. "That divides the long walk better. Then go on to Sahagún tomorrow."

"I thought that was decided. We are not stopping in hostels," I snapped. "Besides I've sent my sleeping bag back."

"What difference does that make? We've walked past camping stores this morning. Sleeping bags are not expensive. Or heavy," Wendy said forcibly.

"Look, I know you haven't given up on your desire to do part of the Camino traditionally by staying in those ancient albergues, but, honestly, Wendy, they are substandard." She shrugged and said nothing. I had a sinking feeling that I would be sleeping in albergues for a while.

Marion and David began to pack up lunch. Mac threw out the water and orange peel. Suddenly my ears began to ache and so did my chin. I was filled with a longing to stop and have another beer rather than continue.

"What's tomorrow look like?" questioned David. "How are your feet, Pat? Mine are sore this morning." I looked over at him and Marion. In the darkness this morning I had seen him limping and had felt his eyes on me.

I didn't answer, although my feet were painful. Marion trudged on beside him.

"As I said before, why don't we stop in Calzadilla tonight and head on to Sahagún tomorrow?" Wendy looked me in the eye, and then offered a compromise. "That way we have a short walk into León and time to see the cathedral."

I started to protest that we'd need a full day at least to see the cathedral and then stopped. I'd take on that battle closer to the day.

"Do you realize that we have walked close to four hundred kilometres? In about twenty days?" I asked.

There was a long silence before Mac replied, "We're doing okay. So let's go ahead with the plan to stay in Calzadilla, go to Sahagún tomorrow, and spend time in León at the cathedral." I felt my heart lighten.

For the remainder of the day, the landscape was flat and monotonous. The close-cropped grass and scrubland offered little relief to the eye. We crossed a bridge over railway tracks and then continued on the typically straight Roman road across the landscape. I could smell the fragrance of thyme as we walked across the dirt path. I counted my steps and called on my guide, Estragon, to break the silence and fill the magnificent sky above me. He fell into step without effort.

I replayed last night's heated debate over walking the meseta. Many of the pilgrims insisted that the meseta was just too flat, had no shade in this heat, and should be missed. We saw them lined up for the bus this morning. They would go on directly to León. Others like us found the meseta beautiful, mystical, and at the very heart of what we were doing— experiencing the Camino in its fullness. The sky was brilliant blue and the horizon seemed so low, barely breaking the surface. Memories of the flat plains of Saskatchewan came back to me. My parents were from the southern part of the province, where the towns were small and the farms were big. Seeding clay soil, waiting for the first green shoots to show, and then watching the sky for rain clouds were all a part of our conversations as we undertook the yearly drive to the small towns where my parents had grown up. There were trips where the thunderheads filled the sky from the horizon to well above our heads. Lightning flashed and thunder rolled. As a child I used to press my face against the window and watch as we sped along just ahead of the raindrops.

I tapped out the rhythm with conviction. My feet were killing me, the blisters were painful, and my pack ground into my shoulders with each step. I squinted at the ball of blinding light called the sun and prayed. It was in the middle of a prayer to a nameless, formless god that I realized my commitment to this walk was deepening. Much of that commitment and the growing strength to continue I owed to the brief but profound walk with my father. I looked around at the stark, unforgiving landscape. Every detail stood out in harsh relief against the immensity of the sky.

I could see a small town off in the distance, perhaps Calzadilla. The land looked more fertile and a small creek ran through a shaded picnic spot. I'd soon be there and join up with the group. I walked faster, eager to see them.

The approach to the town was not welcoming. And by the time I caught up to the others at the entrance to the albergue, I was hurting. My feet were blistered and burning.

"No time to break with tradition," I said with a laugh I didn't feel. "Señor," I called, "we'll have beer." I held up my hand, five fingers displayed.

The headwaiter took one look at us and signalled to the stairs heading to the second floor. As we passed through the dining room, the rapid clip of Spanish punctured the air. It's like guitar music, I thought. People were well dressed—suits, dresses—and sat around tables with sharp white tablecloths. There were carafes of red wine, bread, and olive oil on the tables. As we walked to the stairs, one table stood out from the others. Two people were sitting opposite each other. The woman's hair was pulled back from her face. Her eyes were flashing, the hoop earrings caught the light as she tilted her head, leaning forward and gesturing emphatically. Her red dress clung to her body and its curves. Her companion was a handsome man. His dark skin and black eyes stood out against the white shirt, open at the neck. He was leaning back rocking his chair slightly, almost in rhythm with the voices. Just as I came up beside them, he shouted, "¡Basta!" Upon this command, the restaurant noise stopped immediately. All heads turned to the table. He heaved himself upright, an arm raised, and shoved his wallet into his pocket. She stared at him, lips pulled back in anger, bracelets on her arm jangling. He seized her arm, pulled her to her feet. She lost her balance. He turned, still gripping her arm and walked her to the door.

The headwaiter shouted something that I didn't understand. The man stopped, reached into his pocket, and threw a handful of coins in his direction. The door slammed shut. Silence lingered in the restaurant; then the room was full of Spanish voices, laughter. The evening continued.

"I wonder what that was all about," muttered Mac as we began to walk up the stairs.

"It's obvious it was brewing for a while. That's our drama for today on the Camino, and I'm willing to admit I was scared."

"Ah," said Wendy. "Who knows what may be lurking on the second floor?" The second floor room was crammed with long trestle tables covered in white newsprint. There were carafes of red wine, salt and pepper shakers, and baskets of bread scattered at random down their length. We recognized several other pilgrims and moved along to one of the nearest tables where Franz and Helmut were seated.

"You had a good day?" I asked. I had a vivid image of them walking by me with military precision. As they passed me, Franz had said, "Buen Camino," saluted, and soon they were out of sight.

"Ja, so, it was a good day," said Franz, looking at me speculatively. "And you? Your solitary walk went well?"

"It's been a day of miracles," I said laughingly. "Just one miracle after the other—one foot in front of the other."

"So what does this mean?" Helmut looked puzzled. "I don't understand what you are saying?"

I could feel myself becoming flustered. "Oh, I just mean that the day was good and arriving here with food and wine is a great treat."

Helmut's face broke into a grin. "Now I understand. For me, too, it is good. When you are fifty-six years old it is not easy. And my friend Franz, he keeps a fast pace." He looked warmly at his friend who smiled back.

The food arrived and a comfortable silence settled over us. Geoff, the American, joined us.

"That was a long day," he announced. "And that pack of mine must weigh fifty pounds." When he announced the weight, I felt my shoulders fall.

"You could always leave some of it behind, Geoff—or send it home, you know." I paused.

"Nope, this is my burden, Pat," he said with conviction. "I know I don't need a lot of the stuff, but it's mine and I'm carrying it." He lowered his eyes. "I think I told you that my daughter will meet me one week before we finish the Camino. There might be something she needs. Nope, I'll just carry it. Changing the subject, though, have you noticed how many people are walking alone? I mean without partners?"

"How do you mean partners?" Mac asked.

"Well, I mean a husband or wife. Or a lover. You know there are a lot of singles here."

"You mean like yourself?" I queried.

"Yep!" He wiped off his chin. "Say, this soup is excellent. You should have some, Mac. I know how sick of macaroni you'll soon be. Yes," he continued. "People like me, like Hélène, you Pat, and even like you two guys," he gestured to the two Germans opposite him.

Franz smiled and said, "I have only one bit of advice for you, Geoff. If you find someone, then just remember that what happens on the Camino stays on the Camino."

Geoff blushed. Perspiration showed through his blond thinning hair. "Not me, guys. Count me out. I have a wife back in the States, in Tucson. Nope, I couldn't do that."

"Ach," said Helmut, "you Americans are so serious!" He laughed loudly and several other pilgrims turned to us.

"What's the story?" asked Sebastian. "Perhaps we could all have a laugh."

"Just talking about love on the Camino," said Mac. "I, for one, don't think it's funny. My carnal knowledge diminishes just with the thought of sleeping in a refugio." He and Wendy looked at each other. She reached over and pecked him on the cheek.

"Just think about the fun you'll have regaining lost time, honey," she laughed. "After all, pilgrimages are about a quest."

"And what do you think I'm talking about?" demanded Mac. The table broke into laughter.

The kitchen doors slammed and the waiter arrived with the main course. He slapped them down in front of us with no ceremony.

"Gracias," I tried. He grunted and turned back to the swinging doors.

We left the restaurant near nine that evening. On our way to the refugio, I spotted a small friendly looking bar.

"How's about a brandy to sleep on?" I asked my friends. We ordered three brandies, which arrived in huge snifters.

"I think the challenge will be to drink these and get back to the hostel," Mac remarked.

I groaned. "I'm going back to that refugio—something I said I'd never do—crawl into that sleeping bag, and settle in for the nocturnal anvil chorus. Thank God I kept my ear plugs."

Mac interrupted me. "Tell me, Pat, what do you think about the singles on this Camino? Have you met many?"

"When I think about it, yes. At first, the number of women on their own surprised me. Lots of French, Quebecoises, some Spanish, some English or Dutch."

"Why is that?" Wendy asked. "Have you asked them about their partners?"

"Yes, I do sometimes. If I could summarize, I'd say that their husbands or lovers just aren't interested. Some of the women are Catholics and are on a religious pilgrimage—you know, to help a sick friend, to pray for a departed soul, to find their own salvation. They say their husbands can't get time from work. Yet most of them work, too. So I read between the lines that these men are not interested in walking the Camino. Lots of the women have thought about the Camino for years—just like you and me, Wendy. And then they arrive at a moment when they have to go—regardless of the time of year, of all other barriers. They are simply compelled to head off."

"Come to think of it," said Mac. "I guess there are quite a few guys, too. We just don't think of it as being so unusual when it's a man. No safety issues, you know. And of course," he added with a twinkle in his eye, "we men don't get lonely! Even guys like me who are in touch with our feminine side." Our laughter was warm, inclusive, familiar.

"Well, tomorrow is our last day on the meseta before the foothills. Should be beautiful. But now it's getting late," I said. "Really late for us. It's nine forty-five." We headed off down a side street to the sign for the refugio.

I opened the door slowly to the sight of double-tiered bunks. Huddled forms were outlined in the soft lighting. Several were reading with flashlights, ear buds plugged in. A woman was lying on her back, writing in a notebook held on her knees.

"Home sweet home," I muttered under my breath as I unrolled my new sleeping bag.

CHAPTER 15

BEAUTY

The outline of the far-off hills framed the pink and grey of the early morning light. The sky was barely blue and the clouds were high and wispy. The three of us walked a short distance together.

"You should talk with Franz and get his story," said Wendy. "He's had quite a life. Walked out of his parents' home when he was just sixteen and started to walk around the world. He came back when he was twenty-five. He and Helmut have been best friends since their elementary school. Helmut is married, too, and they have no children. So they are an extended family for Franz's kids. The men do a long walk each year."

I nodded. The image came to mind of Franz and Helmut sitting together—their bodies settled in like a mirror image of each other. "They're very focused," I said. "The only thing they don't do together is write down their observations of the group, at least not in public!"

"What do you think prompted Franz's comment on love?" Mac asked.

I shrugged. "Who knows? Maybe love happened on one of their walks and they knew enough to leave it behind when they went back home."

Wendy looked shocked. "Do you think they're gay?"

"I have no idea whatsoever about that—really none—but I felt that the comments on love were based on his experiences. They had a ring of authenticity."

We walked on in silence and I then sought out my own pace. It felt familiar, welcome, natural. I shifted my pack and thought of Geoff and his fifty pounds of weight. A scene from the movie *The Mission* came to mind. I remembered the heavily frocked priest with his burden of chalices, vestments, and Bibles on his back as he toiled up the mountain trail in the heat. The path was steep and muddy; he was sweating profusely. Suddenly— or at least it seemed to me a sudden decision—he reached into a pocket and pulled out his knife. He slit the rope and watched the bundle of sacred objects bounce down the steep gorge. The sound track gave us the sounds of his breathing and the bumping clashes of the pack as it spiralled down. He stood for a moment staring at the pack and listening to the silence. Then, slowly, he turned back to the trail and began walking. Maybe Geoff is like him, carrying some burden, waiting for a mystical moment in the future.

When I got to Sahagún that evening, Wendy and Mac were sitting in the late afternoon sun. As I walked up to them, I saw the glow of health and outdoor living shining on their faces. Mac was writing in his diary, a part of his evening ritual. Wendy was wearing her evening skirt, her legs stretched out in front of her, her journal in her hand. Seeing them sitting together, each involved in their own thoughts, I could feel the depth of the bond between them, a bond that included their cumulative moments together on the Camino. But, unlike my earlier image of Franz and Helmut who often sat mirroring each other, Mac and Wendy lived separately by respecting each other's need for space and individuality.

As I searched for understanding I remembered German philosopher Husserl's idea of the "life-world." He said that every experience we have becomes a part of us. Many, or even most, of those moments are not available to us. Yet they shape our lives, our reactions, our sense of meaning. Sometimes, he said, the impact of an event brings back past experiences that startle us. But for the most part they go unnoticed. The incident with the man on the path came back to me. It had happened many days ago. And I could still feel the fear and the apprehension if a man passed me not carrying a pack or wearing a coquille. Fear moulded my reactions without my calling on the experience with the exhibitionist. I realized it was still alive in me. Only yesterday a man got out of his car just as I passed by on a lonely stretch of paved road. I instinctively changed my pace, held onto the walking stick tighter, and looked back to see if I was truly alone on the trail. All that without calling on the incident consciously.

I greeted Wendy and Mac and stopped to sit with them a moment. The stone steps of the albergue were cool. I ran my hand along them, feeling the marks of the chisels and hammers of workmen. The colour was soft, like the dried clay fields I had crossed earlier.

In the dining area, the long, hard benches were made of oak. Mac looked at them closely. "Do you know," he asked us, "that oak played a role in the battle between the English and Spanish Armada? It took one thousand oaks to build a ship. Oak is amazingly strong. The English knew they had to be within one hundred metres to penetrate the oak hulls, thus exposing themselves to Spanish fire. After their victory, the English closely monitored the logging of oak for fear of overuse. Still, there are some pieces like this one—old and weathered—to remind us."

Just as we began the meal, Rosita, from Madrid, came into the room. In the few minutes I had walked with her, I had learned that she was doing the walk for her aging mother. She called her regularly because her health was so bad. "But," said Rosita, "she always tells me she will still be there when I return. Some days this makes me happy; other days I resent her insisting that I do the walk for her." She shrugged her shoulders. "What can a person do? She is my mother. This is perhaps the least I can do."

It had been several days since we'd seen each other. When she spotted me at the table she rushed over and gave me a big hug. "Cari," she exclaimed, "you look so good." She stepped back and said appraisingly, "Your body is like new—healthy and fit." She gave me another hug, ignoring my embarrassment. I opened my mouth to speak, but she rushed on. "It is so good to see you. Tomorrow we will walk together. Norbert will be here soon. He is still on Rocinante, his bicycle. He will be glad to see you." Without a pause, she added, "I think he likes you."

I grinned foolishly. All of this was in Spanish and I couldn't get a word in edgewise. She turned quickly and found a free place just behind us. I looked at Wendy and we both smiled.

• • •

We walked out of Sahagún just before seven o'clock the next morning. The sky was in torment and a huge wind whipped the trees and shrubs. The smell of rain and the presence of a storm hung in the air. My jacket rattled in the wind and my hat took off. The walking stick skittered across the cobblestones, but I managed to grab my hat out of mid-air and caught my balance. Like the Chinook winds that leave the Pacific, sweep down the Rocky Mountains, and fill the Alberta plains, this wind knew no bounds. It simply conquered space. I felt invincible! My pace ate up the kilometres. It took little time to walk to the first small town where I saw my friends having coffee in front of a restaurant.

"This is great," I shouted to them. "I don't want to stop!" They looked startled. But I didn't care. A couple of hours later, when the wind had turned to rain, I spotted a little bar. The windows were steamy; damp packs sat outside huddled against the wall. The door banged shut behind me as I pulled up a chair and sat with a group of pilgrims. It wasn't long before the others arrived.

"So, a wet one," Mac said. "We always knew it was a matter of how much rain—not if it rains." I nodded glumly. My pants were soaked; my Gore-Tex jacket had kept the rain out but held in the heat and sweat.

The café con leche warmed my throat and offered a way out of talking. "You want to continue, Pat?" Mac looked anxious.

"Well, what are the options? As far as I can see we can't stay here. León isn't that much farther and I think the sky is lifting."

"I'll order another round of coffees," Marion volunteered, getting up.

"That was quite the pace, Pat," said David. "Thought we'd never catch you!" There was a burst of laughter and I nodded in agreement.

"I love windy weather. It was as though a Chinook had blown in and I just couldn't slow down!"

"Can you keep it up?" Mac asked.

"Don't know, Mac," I replied. "I've never tried so we'll see what this aft brings. Don't get your hopes up. I was built for comfort not for speed." The two men guffawed.

There was movement on the other side of the bar as a group stood up and headed to the door. "Sun's out," said one of the women. "Let's go for it!"

Mac looked around at the group. "Let's us, too! We could make León in an hour and then Pat could have her cathedral in the sun." He grinned down at me, his arm around my shoulders.

We left the bar, found the infamous yellow arrow, and after a short walk chose a spot to cross the N120. We hesitated at the edge of the highway. The cars and transport trucks hurtled by us; the noise of the engines and the speed were daunting. I sat straddling the heavy metal fence for some time. My courage came up in my throat. I looked both ways, gauged the traffic, and ran for the other side. Just then the sun pierced the clouds—a good omen.

We weren't far from the top of a slight elevation. In front of us, shining against the soft grey mist, I could see the outline of the cathedral of León. Its towers, white as milk, beckoned. Behind the cathedral, the shadowy outline of the snow-tipped Montes de León and the Cordillera Cantábrica were visible. I gasped at the beauty spread out before me.

"Wendy," I whispered, "this is awesome. Look at the cathedral! It has practically no hard lines, like a mirage." I turned to look at her. Her eyes were fixed in the distance and she nodded, mute.

We continued along a busy thoroughfare, following yellow arrows and the occasional brass scallop shell embedded into the sidewalk. We arrived shortly at a traffic circle with signs indicating albergues, the city centre, and the cathedral.

"Let's get our accommodation, eat, and head to the cathedral," David announced, turning left.

"Not on your life," I said. "I am not waiting to see this cathedral, particularly not in order to get sleeping accommodation! I'll join you later if you want to stop here." I shifted my pack on my back and started to walk ahead, following a sign indicating the cathedral.

"Just a moment," Marion snapped. "We need some agreement. We are all heading off in different directions." I looked at her and shrugged.

"There's another albergue just on the other side of the cathedral," Wendy said, her guidebook open. "If we take it, we'll be close to the exit for tomorrow morning. Likely worth the extra cost."

I started to protest, then stopped and smiled to myself. First, get to the cathedral, right? Then tomorrow talk everyone into staying longer.

"Great," I said. "That's settled." I turned and followed the sign to the cathedral. We had soon passed the city walls and found ourselves in front of the magnificent Gothic façade.

I had read about the stained glass windows of León and imagined they would be on a par with Burgos. Now that I saw the white stone framing the stained glass I understood that León was unique in its beauty. I went to the side door where groups of people were coming and going. My first steps took me into the darkness. I squinted and looked up. The stained glass windows were radiant as the late afternoon sun poured through them. They cast colours, shadows, and forms on the white stone.

The open design of the cathedral followed the principles of thirteenth-century architecture in France. Its space was open, unencumbered by walls and dividers. This let the light stream across the nave, and the blues and greens pulled my gaze upward. Nearby, a tourist was scanning the ceilings and the windows with binoculars. I envied him.

I looked closely at the glass windows. The panels alternated between portraits of saints and the rich benefactors who had donated the windows. In other windows there were scenes of the craftsmen whose work was also celebrated throughout the cathedral.

Wendy appeared before me, guidebook in hand. "Have you seen the choir stalls? They date from the fifteenth century and have all sorts of amazing imagery! There are personifications of the seven deadly sins and every vice you could imagine! Some nobleman is going to hell for his gambling; a priest was spanking a boy! You name it, it's all here." She grinned, then wandered off across to the chapel where the Gothic tombs were visible.

As I walked on, my surroundings awoke a sense of wonder in me. Not only did beauty surround me, it was embedded in my very being. With each breath my experiences merged with it. I had never seen such colour and design in one cathedral. Mingled with this sense of awe was joy. As so often, I searched for words and was stuck for names to describe the emotions that were part of it.

I saw Mac seated on a bench, staring at the reflected colours above him. It was then that I noticed David and Marion about to leave through the main entrance. I pointed at my watch and Mac nodded in agreement.

The evening air was cool and held a healing grace. We continued in silence to the albergue to get our credenciales stamped, then walked over to the dining hall.

"That was truly one of the most extraordinary visits to a Gothic cathedral I have ever experienced," said David. "We Anglicans just can't hold a candle to this."

At a nearby table, Sebastian lifted his head and joined in the conversation. "Just remember that their art and architecture didn't last forever. It was never viewed separately. After all, at least we learned to separate that which was holy from artifice and representation."

My annoyance flickered hotly. I bit my tongue and changed the subject. "How was your day, Sebastian?" I asked. I gave a sigh of relief as the conversation slid onto traffic and chance encounters with other pilgrims.

It was early when I headed back alone to the small dormitory beside the kitchen. We had put our packs on our bunks to reserve them. I got ready for bed, dressed in my nightshirt, a flashlight on a band around my head, and opened my novel. Reading was not possible. When I shut my eyes, colours, incense, and objects flooded my mind—images of astounding beauty that stayed with me as I slept.

• • •

It was pitch black and overcast when we set out. The entire city was asleep. The morning began as it often did, in a search for the flechas. And, as so often, we could find none. David headed off to the left, peering down a small lane.

"Nope, nothing here," he whispered. Wendy stood under a street lamp, focused on her guidebook. I leaned on my walking stick, the knob comfortable in my palm. There's no point in joining in this search, I thought. Of the five of us, the other four were scurrying around. I shifted my weight, feeling the soreness in my feet from yesterday's walk. It'll be a tough one today. I'll just wait here.

Mac's voice came out as a loud whisper. "I think I've found it," he exclaimed. "Right over here."

"That's not possible," Wendy's voice hissed. "According to the guidebook it's to our right. You haven't found the one that guides us out of town. That one goes back to the albergue. We need to go farther to the right."

"It's right here, David," said Mac, apparently not hearing Wendy. "Big as life." He walked a little farther. "Yes, I can make out another one near that other street lamp." He began walking.

"You're not listening, Mac," Wendy's voice grew louder. "That one goes back to the plaza. The guidebook is really clear—over to the right!" I could see her face, her frown, her eyes narrowed. "Mac," she began again. The white of the book's pages cast an eerie glow in the street light. She walked quickly to the right. Mac and David continued moving to the left, and Marion stood hesitantly in the shadow of the building. I straightened up, pushing a little on the walking stick, and began to follow Wendy. As I walked toward her I could make out a flecha in the semi-darkness.

"Mac," I whispered, "there's one over here." I could make out the silhouette of his shoulders and the rhythm of David's walk. They didn't appear to have heard us.

"Christ!" hissed Wendy. "The bugger never listens to me. Mac! Mac! Pay attention, it's this way."

"What did you say, Wendy?" Mac stopped a little way into the lane opposite us. "You've found a flecha?" He ambled over in our direction.

"Christ," said Wendy, talking to herself. "Whaddaya think, I just talk to make noise? Why is it always the same? This is the story of our relationship. To hell with it." She jabbed her walking stick at the ground and strode off.

I stood between the two of them, walking stick poised in my hand, and grinned awkwardly. "She's right, Mac," I said. "There's the flecha and underneath is written 'Carretera 20,' Highway 20, heading out of town."

"Well, why didn't she say so?" Mac's voice sounded reasonable.

"C'mon, David. Where's Marion? This is it."

We were soon within the sound of traffic and I could hear the rumble of transport trucks. The two couples passed me without talking. Wendy looked pointedly away from Mac. David and Marion were hand in hand.

I could just make out the unlit neon signs in the shop windows, which were closed and dark. It's an industrial area, I realized, as I made out the machines in the gloom of the security lights.

Not too hot this morning. Maybe it'll be a little cooler than yesterday. In yesterday's paper the weatherman had complained about the hotter-than-usual temperatures for September and October. He predicted more wind and rain for today. There were more headlights of cars and trucks as I neared a pedestrian crossing. I could just make out my friends as the first light of the sunrise outlined their movements. The sky began to change. The sun's rays hit the sulfur-coloured clouds as they scudded across the sky. Looks like the day of reckoning from the Bible, a sort of Armageddon, I thought aimlessly, watching the pageant. The wind was cold and unfriendly, prodding away at me. Some time later the cold weather gave up. The warmth of the sun was endearing and my mood brightened.

I was walking down a street near a railway station when I heard someone call out my name. The accent was French. I turned and saw Claudine from Rimouski sitting at a table with Pierre-Yves, Jean-Baptiste, and another man I didn't recognize.

"Hi there! Come on over and join us," she called out. I swung over to the table, dropping my pack with relief, and gave her a hug.

"So good to see you, Claudine. I thought our paths had separated forever. "

"Aha," said Jean-Baptiste. "You never know what may happen on the Camino. Have a beer with us."

I waved to the waiter who shouted back, "Right away."

"Don't count on him to be fast even though he just promised," Claudine said. They exchanged glances and laughed. I could see they had been there for a while. I held out my hand to the stranger. He took it, half stood up, and said in French, "I am Patrick from Toulouse." He immediately began to imitate my accent in French. "How are you, Petula Clark?"

I felt a tingle of annoyance. "That's old, Patrick. It dates you. And I am Canadian, not British," I pronounced it as Breeteesh, imitating the French.

"Then I will call you 'canadienne,'" as he continued to imitate my accent.

The waiter swung the glass of beer over my head. "Three euros," he said almost in my ear.

"It's not important, Pat," said Claudine. "Patrick is a nightclub singer. This sort of thing is part of his trade." I held up my glass to toast with them. Patrick extended his glass to Claudine first.

"Here's to us," he said smiling, his eyes fixed on her.

She blushed slightly and said, "Cheers."

"I think I've seen you on the trail, Patrick," I said. "Weren't you the guy doing a headstand by the side of the road? It's a bit hard to recognize you now but …"

The others joined in the laughter.

He looked solemn. "It is very good for the thinking to do that," he asserted.

"So we can expect some changes in your approach?" I couldn't resist.

"No. Likely not," he said, once again imitating my accent.

Claudine laid her hand on his shoulder. "Let it go," she said. "Let's have another beer."

I noticed that her accent was stronger. That was the effect of the beer, I thought. She was more relaxed. Patrick turned and dropped a kiss on her hand just as it left his shoulder. She blushed again.

Jean-Mi, a Parisian I had met a few days earlier, arrived at that moment. The blue scarf knotted around his neck was wet with perspiration. I watched him walk toward us and thought how he would look at home in his corner of Paris. He had told me that some of his ancestors had walked the Camino during the Inquisition and that he was going to erect a plaque for them.

"Let's stop for a few minutes." His voice had a thin, whiney sound. Anna, his partner, looked at him in annoyance.

"Pas encore!" she protested. "We'll never get to Santiago." He flopped down on a chair.

"There's a chair over here, Anna," I said. "I'm off." I hugged Claudine. "See you again, I hope, but who knows? Jean-Baptiste is right. On the Camino you just never know. See you, Patrick." He waved with his free hand as he lifted the beer glass to his lips.

I walked on alone, carrying the images of León's cathedral around my heart like a rosary. The forms and colours of its architecture and windows lifted me away from the everyday. I strode on, swinging my walking stick and watching the clouds in the pale blue sky and the white-tipped mountains of Cantabria, which ran parallel to the clouds. Holding the walking stick in both hands, I bumped it against my thighs. My chant—body-mind-body-spirit-body-heart—lifted the sense of fatigue. The rhythm of the chant led to calmness and connection. Living in my pace was a ritual, a prayer, and it brought peace and centredness.

CHAPTER 16

LOVE ON THE CAMINO

In Astorga, the two couples were sitting in the shade of a bar near the entrance to the city. Mac had his guidebook open and the others were leaning over him. "There you are, Pat," he said. "We're just having a look at the route from here. We'll be challenged by several mountain passes in the next week or so."

I dropped my pack and joined them, calling to the waiter, "Una cerveza, por favor."

Mac ran his finger along the map. "As you can see we are likely out of the meseta tomorrow and into Rabanal. After that it's tougher, mountain country."

I peered more closely at the map. "Don't forget we're stopping at the chocolate factory here, Mac!" I announced. "We must not forget how culture is formed. Vámonos, mis amigos. We need an albergue and I, for one, need a shower."

We struck out around seven the next morning before the sun became a constant and difficult companion. At midday, I sat perched on a bale of hay. It was the only place to sit in this treeless landscape. Heat waves rose along the horizon. The sun was soaking into my neck and hands inch by inch. I knew the night would bring little relief. My throat was dry and the apple I had just finished hadn't made much of a difference. I heard the murmur of French voices and looked back down the trail. It was Claudine and Patrick deep in conversation. Although the path was rough in places, they were looking at each other and maintaining their momentum. It was not only their eyes that made contact, their bodies seemed to twist toward each other, moving, changing, searching. There was no laughter, no signs of levity, just deep engagement. Could love happen on this dry, barren, huge landscape? Well, why not? I reasoned. In any case, it was not for me to question. They stopped, we chatted briefly. They left almost immediately.

Claudine called over her shoulder. "We'll be in Riego de Ambrós tomorrow. Maybe we'll see you."

Patrick turned, looked at her, and said something I didn't hear. She smiled again.

"I have a serious question for you, Pat," Wendy said as I walked into the bar that evening. "Have you seen Patrick and Claudine?"

"Yes," I replied, knowing where the conversation would lead us.

"Do you think something is going on? Isn't she married? What's up?"

I felt the irritation in my shoulders. "I don't know if something is going on. What gives you that idea? And who cares, anyway?"

Wendy looked at me closely. "Well, I suppose you're right, but isn't it interesting? I mean, an affair." She paused significantly.

"Une affaire d'amour," I said. "It's the everyday miracle. People meet and fall in love regardless of the circumstances. That's the great thing about love. It happens."

"But," Mac picked up the questioning, "what about her husband? I mean ..."

"He's back home in Rimouski, not here. So what's the problem? Or is there one? What makes up a private life? Can you have one when you're married? Like your own secrets? Or do you have to share everything?" My voice sounded querulous to my ears.

There was a silence.

"Think I'll have another beer," I said, calling to the waiter.

To myself, I admitted that the relationship seemed to have changed since I last saw them in the café. Today's conversation looked as if it had gone on for a while and it seemed somehow intimate. Privilege was the word that came to mind. It was a privilege to see love happen—if it was love. And what did Nietzsche say? You can't say yes to love without saying yes to pain?

It was early the next morning in a small café across from our albergue when I saw them again. They walked in together, not touching physically, not holding hands, but together. Claudine was radiant.

"Hi there," she said as she kissed me on the cheek and gave me a hug. She was smiling and I noticed for the first time that she had a small dimple. Patrick also kissed me. "Bonjour," he said, still imitating my accent.

I gave a tug to a strand of his hair. "And how about you, you crusty old Frenchman. Things going okay?" We laughed together.

"What are you saying?" asked Wendy.

"He's doing his usual imitation of my accent. God, the French mania for perfection is enough to drive a person 'round the bend. They are constantly reminding us that French is the world's best language and they are its only true speakers!" I snorted.

Claudine grinned at me. "It's true. They are hard on us, too, even though we are francophone." Her Quebecois accent was not as strong this morning. She sounded more like Patrick to my ears. It's a sign of belonging, I thought, this unconscious imitation of posture or a gesture or using the same turn of phrase. There was a sort of repose in their movements, their talk paced and intimate. They ordered cappuccinos and croissants. They had all the time in the world.

Mac's voice reminded me that we didn't. "Well, it's nearly eight," he said significantly. Wendy and I picked up our packs, said goodbye, and headed out into the soft light of early morning.

"Well," said Wendy, her green eyes glinting, "that's pretty clear. They came from the same direction. Too early for that to be a coincidence!"

The sight of them was imprinted on my mind. "Isn't love beautiful— no, aren't people in love radiant?" I said. "Love beautifies the plainest of us."

Mac looked at me with amusement. "I didn't know you were such a romantic, Pat. I'd just say they're having an affair!" We all laughed.

"That's true, too. But when I saw them this morning I thought of love as the everyday miracle. It just happens, without us looking for it. It complicates, baffles, and contradicts reality. It touches us with grace."

"Enough, you two," Wendy said. "We have a Camino of thirty-two kilometres today. Save some of that energy."

Our familiar pattern set in. I dropped back, watching them walk together as they pulled away from me. His head was bent down toward her, his body on a slight angle. I could see her profile as she looked up at him. Their pace was quick and their legs moved in unison.

The morning encounter had left me mellow and filled with happiness. Regardless of how it ended, this was right for them. A scene from an old Bergman movie came back to me. It was a black and white film and the scene I remembered was in silhouette. It was the time of the black plague. People were dancing in single file, hands outstretched to each other as they turned and kept time with the rhythm. The setting sun outlined their bodies, but their faces were in the shadow, anonymous. Their movements were light and instinctive. No one was out of step or out of time as they wove a garland across the ridge, disappearing into a forest—the end of their lives. That's what the Camino felt like today. Somehow we were in rhythm, in sync, and we touched each other ever so lightly as we moved along. In some mysterious way we had outlines, but the details, the colours, the textures were not obvious. Maybe love was like that. Like a mysterious rhythm that couldn't be played but could be followed if you were open to it.

Garth came to mind. I recalled how we had fallen in love. Then everything had stopped abruptly, unpredictably. Like being amputated from a life source. It had been one soul in two bodies and dividing the soul was like a painful death. I realized that my breathing had become shallow and I had nearly stopped at the roadside. Around me, morning activities were starting. I was surrounded by birdsong, tractors in the fields, the occasional hawk drifting on updrafts. I shifted the pack, breathed in deeply and sighed. In my heart I held Claudine and Patrick close. I wished them—. No, that action distanced me from them. I felt a part of them, in the love and, in the long run, likely in the pain.

The breeze was gentle that morning. It lifted my hair slightly as it passed. With it came the smells of wood smoke, of greenery, and of fresh mown hay—the fragrances of autumn in Galicia.

Three old women were standing gossiping as I entered Molinaseca. They were short, gnarled like the trees behind them. Their aprons were tucked up at the corner but still covered most of their dresses. They stood close together each wearing rough-hewn wooden clogs with heels. I heard the sound of their laughter as I drew closer. The one with a knotted headscarf was talking rapidly. Her hands carved the space in front of her and underlined a good story. As I passed by, her grin was infectious. I stopped. Their smiles showed a few missing teeth.

"How are things?" I asked.

One of them nodded. "Bien" was the reply.

"I have never seen shoes like this before." I spoke in Spanish and pointed to their clogs. "Why do you have heels like that?"

The one who was carrying a small sack of field vegetables answered. "When you are herding pigs in Galicia and it rains, these help with the footing," she explained.

"Did you make them yourselves?" I asked, curious to know more.

All three laughed out loud. "Never! Not a job for us señoras," said the spokeswoman. "I tell my husband what to do—and just look, señora," she gestured to their feet, "these are the results of my orders." They all laughed again. The breeze picked up slightly as we moved apart.

"Buen Camino," they called back over their shoulders.

"Gracias, señoras," I answered. "See you again some time!"

The breeze was warm and companionable, like a Chinook. I had spent so many days in the mountains on horseback. Even as I walked along I could feel the rhythm of Prince, my quarter horse.

"He's a horse you can spoil and not ruin," said Colin when he sold me the horse twenty years ago. "And on top of that, you can count on him one hundred percent in the mountains."

And that had been so true. I remembered how it felt as he tucked his back quarters under to climb up steep trails, sliding on loose rocks, but throughout it all his sense of balance, his ears turned back as he listened to me. Our relationship with horses is unique, I thought to myself. They carry us, know us from our balance, our harmony with them. The energy flows between us—that's the form of communication. They are so big and overbearing yet so compliant, so biddable. Even Indio had those qualities. I could sense him walking with me in this harsh dry land, his head tilted slightly toward me, his shoulder just behind my body, alert, responsive to every move I made. His blue eye looked soft and concerned, his nose turned in close to my waist. He shortened his stride slightly to accommodate my pace. The breeze lifted his curly white mane. Such splendid markings, I thought. In the half of his face that was black there was an indigo eye and the other half was white with a large spot of mascara around his dark brown eye. His black tail floated out behind him, nearly touching the ground. If Prince was my constant companion and caregiver, Indio was my teacher. His fear and anxiety around new people and places made him a challenge to ride.

"It's in his nature to be oppositional," Kevin had said. "He lives in opposition to being ridden, to being shod—just about everything. That's just him. It'll take a lot of time to ride him like you want to. But it will be worth it."

So the lessons had begun. There were lessons for a childless woman in fear, in courage, in persistence, and in loving a living being when they least deserve it.

The hugeness of the land pressed in on my musings. I listened to its warm westerly wind and birdsong. It had been a day like today the first time Indio bucked. I felt it again in the very core of my body, heard my voice thin with dread. I had dismounted in fear. He was on the verge of misbehaving so I walked him back to the arena before it happened. At one point, I had turned to look at him. He was licking his lips and had the sort of look we get when we've won the fight. How dare he? I grabbed his halter and lunge rope and led him back to the corral. I worked him hard until there wasn't a dry spot on his body. I put the bridle back on and rode him out into the field. He was calm, didn't shy at the gatepost as he generally did. He trotted peacefully, cantered, then we went back to the arena. I ran the cool water over his back and down his legs. He lowered his head and looked me in the eye. Spontaneously, I hugged him, his wet coat and dripping mane soaked into me. He nickered softly. Yes, I thought, one day we would understand each other, but who knows?

My thoughts turned back to Prince. He was still a handsome horse. I could imagine his eyes on me, the soft, slightly worried eyes of a caregiver horse. He was happy now to fit in; his gait had slowed. Our time together was growing shorter. I couldn't imagine my life without him. It will be a day of such sorrow and pain.

The next town was baking in the sun when I crossed the plaza to a small coffee bar. The bartender looked at me closely as I took off my sunglasses.

"A double macchiato, señora?" he asked.

That's what I need, I thought to myself as I nodded to him, something strong to change my thoughts. We talked briefly in Spanish about the weather, the unseasonable heat, the crops just harvested. He turned back to the tray and continued to dry glasses. He had strong, tanned hands with thick black hair on them. The rhythm of turning the glass, running the towel inside it, and setting it in its place on the counter somehow reassured me. The room was filled with sunlight and the buzz of flies. I squinted outside to the plaza. Several pilgrims were just coming across to my bar. I recognized Norbert on his bicycle Rocinante. His beret was set at a jaunty angle. When he saw me, he called out, "¿Qué tal, Patricia?" and smiled warmly.

I pulled up a chair beside me. He stowed his bicycle in clear view and sat down. His Spanish was a treat to listen to.

"Tell me, how did you learn such wonderful Spanish, Norbert? It's your third language, right?"

"Yes," he replied, his eyes growing soft with the memory. "I was only eighteen and came to Spain for no real reason, just to travel. Barcelona was the first city that I stopped in." He paused and put sugar in his coffee. "I found a hostel near the centre of the city. And it was there, at the very moment when I walked into the place, that I heard my first Spanish phrase and fell instantly in love. I was transfixed by the sound and the rhythm of the language." He smiled at the memory.

"I can just imagine you stopping at the door, caught up in the sounds of a new language," I said.

He ignored my comment and continued. "I started out by just sitting at a table in a bar and listening to the sounds. Slowly words emerged, then verbs, then sentences. I am still learning to speak better, of course. Once a love affair starts it never finishes. There is always something new to learn." A shadow of sadness crossed his face and I remembered that his partner had not wanted to come to Spain with him. She had stayed back in Toronto.

He turned resolutely to me and said, "You, too, you love Spanish. You speak well, although there is much for you to learn." Spoken as a true teacher, I thought. A compliment is always accompanied by a plan for improvement.

"You're right, Norbert. I have much to learn. I, too, fell in love with the language, but at university. My first class was taught by a Polish professor, Bohdan Plascatcz, who spoke nine languages fluently. I still remember some of the stories he told us. I think I could still quote them verbatim they were so interesting."

We sat quietly for some time. "Yes, well," he said thoughtfully, "that is how language shapes our lives, how we make sense out of situations like this one." He gestured around the bar. In one corner was a couple speaking German, in another corner a lone pilgrim reading a book in Spanish. The town mongrel was flaked out at the door, flies droning monotonously. Norbert's bike was gleaming in the sun.

"Best I go. Rocinante is getting hot—soon I won't be able to climb on her back!" He leaned over and kissed me on the cheek. "Have a good day, Patricia," he said. "Salud, pesetas y amor—what more could we ask for?"

He swung over the crossbar of the bicycle and, wobbling slightly, crossed the plaza and took a left at the yellow arrow.

I sat for a few more minutes, my thoughts turning inward. Norbert had talked about how we shape our lives with different languages. I could see that the language of horses had also shaped my world. It was a communication that had no words, no verb tenses, but the seamless flow of energy and commitment. Often the world of horses went unread and unheard. The ignorance surrounding their language could not negate its existence. For those with the courage, dialogue was possible. In my brief and limited experience, sometimes the communication was poetic, other times the language of the heart, and at times humorous. Through all the many and variable forms flowed some desire to work with us humans, to collaborate, to be partners in shaping common ground.

I found the familiar flecha and followed Norbert's bicycle track in the dirt until it disappeared on the gravel and stones. The arrows led me to another small town by mid-afternoon. The shop on the plaza was open and the air inside was cool. My energy had sunk and I went in looking for chocolate bars and almonds. The shelves were stacked with tinned food and drinks. As I scanned them looking for food, I saw the baskets. They were woven of rough material; the colours were soft brown, worn reds, and black. Each had its own shape. I picked one up and turned it over. I could just make out the faded signature on the bottom. The name was "Esperanza." I could see her in my mind's eye: dark eyed, small, threading the needle and weaving the colours. The baskets were not large and seemed designed for carrying small objects. I held one up in front of my eyes against the light streaming in the door. I could see the texture and feel its indefinite shape shift and flex as I turned it in my hand. It was not solid but pliant to the touch and responsive to its own weight.

"What are these for?" I asked the shopkeeper. "Who makes them? Someone near here?"

He squinted at me for a moment. "Señora, they are made by the women in a small town not far from here." He waved his hand to the west. "It is an ancient craft, weaving, and one that the women of that valley have always done. They're from Galicia." He shrugged his indifference. "What more can I say? I don't speak their dialect very well. I just know that they have always made them. They use them for collecting the mushrooms in the spring. You can see that they are made for small things, not big stuff like potatoes."

He rang up my purchases and took the bill I held out to him. "Are you going to buy one? The last buyer was also a pilgrim."

I shook my head. "I don't want to carry the extra weight." I walked out of the store into the heat and the dagger-like sunlight. I thought of those women using the baskets as containers for spring mushrooms. They would be chanterelles—light, pungent chanterelles. I could imagine them held in the circle of the basket, a sort of embrace really. Like the presence of my father the day I fell—or the contact between Claudine and Patrick that had stayed with me all day. There are spaces in each embrace, I thought. The edges are defined but open to negotiation; the feelings of an embrace are feelings of inclusion and safety. Ursula Le Guin says that we made baskets long before we learned how to kill animals with stones and sticks. I thought of Esperanza in her home weaving. Even her name seemed appropriate: Esperanza—hope.

It was late when I arrived in Ponferrada, a modern city built on the ruins of the Celts, Romans, and Visigoths over the centuries. Another pilgrim encouraged me to see the Castle of the Templars and visit the statue of Virgin of the Oak, a small statue still embedded in the original tree trunk. I skipped it all and went to a bar near the plaza where I found our group with Marcel, a French Canadian. They were heading to an outdoor table, each with a beer in hand.

"How's your day been?" I asked. Immediately the exchange of stories started. "Did anyone go into the little shop near the brick refugio? Did you buy any baskets?" I asked. They shook their heads.

"Did you buy anything?" Marion asked.

I grinned, nudging the pack with my foot. "You can count on it—nothing more needed in this. It has too much in it already—and some of it weighs nothing!" We all laughed. Sending small items home had been part of the first days of the Camino. "What I saw and really liked were some small hand-woven baskets of soft, faded colours, likely made in their homes. They're for harvesting mushrooms in the spring."

Marcel looked interested. "I wish I had seen them," he said. "I'd send them back to Chicoutimi to my mother. She loves baskets, says they remind her of picking berries as a child, using the birch bark baskets of the Indians." He looked at us. "So the women do that here, too. There's an old saying: Plus ça change, plus c'est la même chose."

"The French have a lot of sayings," commented Mac.

"And that's how we get them. We borrow them! Thank God for the French," I said jokingly.

The air outside was cooling off and the sun was sinking in the west. I relaxed and raised my feet up on the low bench beside me. What a wonderful day, I thought. I wish this trip would never end. I realized, suddenly, that this "trip"—or, to be more exact, the journey—would end only when I met death on whatever day or date.

I grinned at my companions. "How's about another toast, a Jewish one? 'La heim,' to life!" We raised our glasses.

"You're mellow tonight, Pat," said Wendy as we got up. I nodded. It was true. As Wendy and Mac and I headed to the albergue I thought about how we always walked together in the towns we visited. Our paces were compatible in many ways. It was only during the daytime that pace separated us. What that time apart had come to mean for me was the time and ease of being part of any world I sought out. I took my time, ambling and chatting, loving the moments, the Spanish people, my own pace.

The three of us walked by a bar full of pilgrims who looked over, recognized us, and waved. We were delighted to be in that little town, following an ancient path, sharing the same experiences.

The next morning, I closed the door softly making sure I heard the click as it shut. The night light in the hallway outlined our shapes as we walked carefully down the stairs. I could just make out my watch.

"It's ten to seven," I whispered to Wendy.

"Okay," she said. "Let's grab a coffee in that little restaurant we saw on the plaza."

•　•　•

The morning air was cool and crisp. There was a slight frost on some of the cobblestones. Across the plaza I could see the light of the restaurant and people drinking coffee.

As we walked in, we found David and Marion sitting at a table. Her face was dusted with the icing sugar of a breakfast cake. David turned to us, beaming, the light glinting off his glasses.

"Hola, pilgrims," he said jovially.

Mac waved and said, "What do you two want?"

"Café con leche," said Wendy, and I added, "Me, too."

I swung my pack off and set it up against the wall near the door. There were already other packs in the shadows and I could see their white scallop shells. The fragrance of coffee, the sight of it steaming in the bowls was a fine beginning to the day. We sat quietly, stirring the lattes and half listening to the sound of sleepy voices. Outside in the blackness I could just make out a couple crossing the plaza. As they arrived into the circle of light, I recognized the Argentinians I had met two weeks ago. I could see a rhythm in their walk, a new-found ease. When I first met them, I thought that Carlos wouldn't make it. He was sweating profusely, limping, and whining. His wife, in her jaunty hat, was striding along ahead of him. She had ignored him as they stopped in the bar. She had talked and laughed with the women, flirted with a couple of the men, and then left. I wasn't sure if she knew—or cared—that he left when she did. This morning, they came in together. Their movements were in sync, their faces calm and relaxed.

I called out, "Hola, fellow travellers."

Carlos turned and smiled, then came over to the table.

"Isn't it marvellous?" he asked. "I am so glad we came, aren't you, my love?"

She kissed his cheek. "Sí, sí, Carlos." She smiled openly at me. "Next year, we come back. We have not the time to finish—so next year!"

"Pat," said Wendy. "Just look." She pointed to the wall behind the bar counter. "See the poster? It says Santiago, 217 kilometres." I peered at it closely. There was the familiar pilgrim form, a man striding along with a gourd attached to his staff, his jerkin swinging, belted with a rope at the waist. "That," she said, "is do-able. We'll be in Santiago—well, how long will it take, Mac?"

Mac looked at the sign. "Well, our pace is about twenty-five kilometres a day. So that's ten days or so." A strange look passed over his face. "My God, we're more than two-thirds of the way there. We'll make it. Right, Pat?"

I could find nothing to say. I suddenly saw the end of the Camino before us. That would mean—so many images flooded my mind: pictures of the cathedrals, taking the bus to Santander, being back in Calgary, not being with Mac and Wendy or David and Marion, all the other people I'd walked with. I looked at my companions. We had done so well since those early days, since those talks in Calgary about walking the Camino. How naïve we were and how certain of success, with no idea of what it would take. On the one hand, I remembered the fear and uncertainty and, on the other, walking in my father's presence, knowing with absolute certainty I'd walk it all.

"Okay, you guys, enough of this lolling about. Are we walking or aren't we?" I asked as I stood up abruptly and headed for the door. "Let's do it! If we don't start walking we'll never get there," I grinned at them.

Chairs scraped back and packs swung in the air as we headed out into the first glimpses of the sunrise. The sky turned pink and golden, wisps of clouds caught the early rays. The horizon was tangerine, the sky above us dusky mauves. My heart soared at the sight of the new day. I could hear the boots of my friends on the gravel; I felt the presence of others gaining on us. All of this in silence, heads down, eyes inward. I felt that we were waiting for permission. Permission for what? To be fully alive, to feel the joy of being here, the sense of pace, and that lightness of here and now as the only place to be.

CHAPTER 17

THE RAINS OF GALICIA

The next morning, I heard the murmur of voices and the click of metal fasteners on backpacks. I opened my eyes reluctantly, groaned, and slumped back on my makeshift pillow. It was far too dark; the clock had to be wrong. I watched other pilgrims through half-open eyes. Their movements were slow, lethargic. One of them rummaged through his pack and pulled out a rain jacket. It was then that I heard the rain on the stone roof and the rattle of the shutters as gusts of wind shook them viciously. I curled up deeper in my sleeping bag. A rainy day. Why get up? We didn't need the whole day to get to Villafranca. From the bunk below me I heard Wendy ask, "What time is it?" Mac's sleepy voice replied, "Time to get going."

It was bitterly cold, wet, and blustery when we stepped out of the albergue. Across the plaza, lights shone through a window, warm and golden on the stones. Without talking we moved as one to the café, heads down, hands holding our hoods in place. We shook off the rain on our jackets, ordered coffee, drank slowly, and said nothing. Looking across the room I saw our reflection in a large tarnished mirror. We looked like refugees waiting for the right moment to flee for safety. David and Marion came in, peering around the room till they found us.

We left soon after, behind a small group of pilgrims. In no time the rain worsened. The fog was thick as we began to climb to the first pass. The vegetation wrapped around my pant legs, soggy and clinging; the puddles just deep enough to get in through the lace holes of my boots. I gave up stepping over puddles and felt the squish of my wet woollen socks as I walked. Along the path, deep in the vegetation, there was the occasional heather in bloom and some beautiful tall pink flowers that resembled crocus blossoms.

Then another gust of sleet would drive through my rain gear and I would shiver with cold. It reminded me of a day of cross-country skiing in the Rocky Mountains with a small group of friends: the weather had turned ugly and we were without adequate clothing. The wind was at gale force when I turned to help out a visitor from Germany behind me. His plastic cape had come loose and whipped out above and behind him. He looked at me and said, "How I wish I wasn't here!" At that time it had sounded plaintive, but looking back, I now heard his desperation.

It took several frigid, miserable hours before we stopped for lunch in a small restaurant, the windows of which were so foggy we couldn't see in. The door swung open as Mac pushed on it, revealing a wet, pathetic group of pilgrims hunched over cups of coffee. The room was packed. It was Sunday, so there were plenty of "car" pilgrims who were dry and tidy compared to us.

"This is really stupid," I said, irritated. "We don't have the right clothes, we are soaked, and we have nothing to change into. How could we be so ill-prepared?"

David turned toward me. He was wearing his hat with the corks attached to the brim, but it had taken on a new angle and was sagging severely. Rain ran along his forehead and down through his beard. His soaked sleeves hung out of his jacket and dragged on the table. "This is the wrong time to complain, Patricia," he announced. "We are here with what we have and there's nothing we can do."

I looked at him with sincere dislike. "That's really helpful, David," I said sarcastically. "What'll I do with that advice?"

His mouth opened as though to speak, but he thought the better of it. I stirred my coffee, the spoon hitting the sides of the mug. Then Wendy spoke up, "Why don't you use your energy to keep on at that pace you've been setting? It's the strongest I've seen you."

I decided to say nothing. My anger ran high as I thought of all the times when forward thinking had made the difference in similar situations. This was not one of those times. I felt responsible and angry. I should have listened to Geoff's advice on rain gear. I had been so confident that we wouldn't see a lot of rain.

At that moment, another pilgrim dripped into the room. His hair ran with rivulets of rain, his jacket was soaked, his pack huge and lopsided. He flopped down on a chair. His eyes rolled in anger and he shouted, "I'm exhausted; I can't do anymore." He was speaking Spanish. We all looked at him in alarm. He pounded the table.

"God, I am so tired." His voice was almost a sob now.

Dumfounded, we said nothing. Then I had an inspiration. "I beg your pardon," I said. "I am thinking of hiring a taxi for my pack. Perhaps you would like to share the cost and take the taxi or put your pack—"

His laughter was maniacal. "Me, take a taxi? Me, pay for it? I can walk! I can walk!" He shouted several times, pointing at me and laughing. "You, on the other hand ..." He went on in a Spanish I didn't understand.

The bartender looked seriously alarmed. He put down the towel and began to walk out from behind the bar. "Señor," he said. "Señor!" The man sat down abruptly, his head hanging.

We got up quickly in the distraction and headed out the door. He shouted something at me, angry again.

I turned and yelled, "Asshole."

"Pat," said Wendy, in shock. "You shouldn't say things like that."

As the door closed I could hear the Spaniards laughing. Some words, I thought, are international. The man stood at the window staring after me. I glared back at him, moving sideways to miss a puddle as I followed my friends.

Outside, the rain continued in earnest. It pelted down; it ran down the cobblestones; it invaded my jacket. The wind lashed at my body. I staggered and nearly lost my balance.

Bright droplets of rain clung to the green vegetation transforming our path along the bottom of the valley. There was water everywhere creating ponds, flowing in streams, softening the harsh lines of the steep valley walls. The valley was criss-crossed with fences made of large rocks to keep in cattle. It reminded me of the Isle of Skye where stones appear to be the only natural resource available for building houses, fences, and roads. I met gnarled old men wearing tweed caps who could have just left a pub anywhere in Ireland. No wonder they say that the Irish came from Spain!

Water came in the form of rain, of fog, and of streams shaping the landscape, and announced itself in my life. It was inside my boots, in my pockets, in my hood. I slogged on miserably, my head down, feet slipping on rocks, the walking stick next to useless.

The path began to climb along a stand of tall trees. Big drops of rain hit my face; I tightened my hold on the hood. The wind picked up the rain and turned it into gusts of water. My hair in front of the hood was soaked. Blinking as the water ran down my face and into the collar of the jacket, I pulled the hood up tighter, my hands freezing in the rain. My boots splashed through the puddles that had appeared without warning.

It was then that I heard the rhythm of galloping horses. I turned and saw four horsemen advancing rapidly toward me. The horsemen of the apocalypse, I thought. The horses were Andalusians. They moved with energy and conviction, the large hooves leaving imprints on the path. Their grey coats were streaked with foam, manes flattened against their necks. As they came closer I could see their wild eyes rolling in their heads. The riders' cloaks billowed with the wind. They were making efforts to hold the horses back. Suddenly, there was a bolt of lightning. One of the horses shied and neighed anxiously. As the lead rider passed he nodded grimly to me. I felt my hand rise to salute him. God, I would love to change places, to find myself astride such a magnificent horse. They ploughed by me and disappeared into the forest on the other side of the highway.

The image of Indio came to me. If he were here, he'd be reacting to the rain and the storm. I could imagine his stride, his high spirits, and my hands in contact with his energy. I wished I were on horseback. Abruptly, the wind swung in a new direction, the rain pelted against my back. I huddled into my hood trying desperately to stay warm.

It was mid-afternoon before the storm abated. We walked under heavy clouds with the occasional outbreaks of sunlight that made the moisture-laden grass and trees sparkle with diamonds.

David and I were walking together as we sometimes did at the end of a day. Our pace was slow and our talk chatty. After a moment of silence, he said, mostly to himself, "I'm still so disappointed. I wanted to find a deeper sense of God and it hasn't happened."

I looked over at him. His profile was downturned, framed by the brim of his swag hat. We walked on in step; the silence lengthened. "I told you yesterday about our group raising money for our church back in Mildura, didn't I? We're building a fine church—simple, but a solid statement of the Anglican presence in our town." I nodded. He looked into my eyes. "You don't have this challenge, do you?"

"Not really, David. I'm not much of a churchgoer. But I think I understand what you are searching for."

"But you seem quite—how should I say—focused on something bigger?"

"Yes, but for me, it's not a person but rather a sense of spirituality, of joy. A lot of that sense comes from the beauty around us and the contact with other pilgrims."

"I don't get it, Pat. That sounds irreligious to me."

We walked on in step. What could I share with him?

"David," I began tentatively "I could tell you about an incident that changed my life, an image that I carry in my heart."

We had stopped walking and stood looking at each other. Slowly he nodded.

"It happened some years ago when I lived in Perth, Western Australia. I had made the decision to leave Canada, my family, my job, and to work on the issue of women in leadership, which I thought was so important."

I paused, sensing his discomfort, but decided to continue. "I knew that such a life-changing transition would demand all my energy and experience. So I sometimes went to see a masseuse, Susan, who did deep tissue work. One day during a session, I had a vision. A slender tube-like form of the purest soft blue came to me. My eyes were closed, but I could see it vividly on my inner eye. The form was alive with energy. In some places it was marred by what looked like rust, or maybe corrosion. I could see, nonetheless, that it was a portrait of my life—with moments of sorrow, loss, alienation. At its very centre was a radiant blue form of hope, belonging, and love. There, that day, in the semi-dark, a sense of wholeness settled deep in my body. This shimmering form represented—actually was—my life." I recalled Susan's voice as she talked me through the experience.

The afternoon light had changed and the land stood clear, trees rising to meet the now gentle sky. A hawk circled, low to the ground, his wings steady, his head bent to search for food. David looked askance. "Is this what gives you faith?" he asked abruptly. "This image, this vague memory of some massage?"

I nodded wordlessly. "It's not the only insight, but for me it is a key to understanding spirituality. It happened when I needed to believe in something, in some larger picture. At the moment of need, it came to me. It came without calling on it." We looked at each other. The gulf widened; the silence deepened.

"David," I said quietly. "We aren't talking about God as your group does. We are talking about the essence—for me—of spirituality."

We started walking again. The rhythm of our pace lengthened. I knew the risk I had taken by even talking about it. I held the image of blue light close to my heart. I remembered its strength and the flow of emotions. Any desire to defend or explain it fell away.

We walked in unison until David said, "Well, I'll catch up to Marion. See you this evening."

I picked up my walking stick in both hands. It swung in rhythm with my pace, floating in my hands. The stick bounced off my thighs as they moved back and forth. I shifted my pack, letting my shoulders drop and relax. I looked up along the horizon to a curve of a hill that was a faded brown and recently tilled. My chant was simple: mind, body, heart, soul. The walking stick picked up the tempo. As if dictated, the patterns changed, the pace grew stronger. I let go of the risk I had felt. Inside arose a sense of well-being.

I called upon the guide, who led me to the place of fire. I saw again the wise, soft, solemn brown eyes. His words held the same message: "You are where you should be and you are doing what you need to do. Don't fret about the end of the Camino. All things come to an end. Life does not stop. Stay in your power, which is joy and love."

Energy surged. I walked a little faster, held my stick in my right hand. It swung in rhythm with my left foot, each touching the ground at the same time. The image of the guide slid away.

It was a relief when I got to the bottom of the hill and the paved road came to an end. I turned left and headed down the quiet, tree-lined track that wound its way to Villafranca del Bierzo. Villafranca was lovely, sitting on a river, the Río Burbia, and in clear sight of the mountains. There were signs on the road for Ave Fénix, reputed to be the best of the albergues on the Camino.

I walked past beautiful houses on narrow picturesque streets just as the first drops started to fall again. Almost immediately the rain pelted down. I pulled my rain jacket out of my pack and wrapped myself in it. What a miserable day, I thought.

When I finally arrived at Ave Fénix I found my friends huddled together on a porch-like deck. "Bloody cold," Mac said. "Let's find a bar and have a drink."

"Before you do," a man in the albergue called out in English, "book in over here so I know if I'm full." We stopped and went to the rudimentary bar barely under the protection of the roof. He stuck out his hand. "I'm called Jesús—Sosus to you!" His laugh was loud and welcoming. "Sign here real quick. I'll find you some red wine. There is a lot in the cellar—and I have something for you to eat. No need to go out in this rain."

We looked at each other, put down our packs, and sat in the half-sheltered area to drink a glass of red. Marion looked exhausted. The brim of her hat sagged and her glasses had slid along her nose. "We may not see much of the trail on this stretch," she commented. "I talked to a couple who said the forecast was bad for another three days." I groaned.

Sosus came back carrying another carafe of wine. "Now," he

announced loudly so that all could hear. "I have rules which you must obey." Mac looked significantly at Wendy and me.

"Here's the story. You cannot get up before seven o'clock in the morning. I don't care how much you want to start before; seven is it. I enforce that." Then he looked pointedly at each of us, meeting our gaze. "Those of you who are more than forty years old must sleep in a room on the second floor. Up there you are near the toilets." He pointed up the stairs to an area where we could just make out a few sleeping figures on bunks. "Those are my house rules. No questions." He turned and lifted the door of the cellar to pull out another bottle of wine. "If you have sore muscles, this fixes them." He flexed his muscles and laughed heartily. "You be okay here with Sosus." He made fists and beat his broad chest, laughing again. He turned and walked back into the albergue against the hill.

"Lucky we're stopping here," said Mac. "Villafranca is the perfect spot before we give O Cebreiro a go."

"It won't be so good if this weather stays the same," I commented. "We'll bloody well freeze. I'm taking out my big orange garbage bags and wearing them instead of my rain pants."

Wendy looked at me, her green eyes twinkling. "I dare you to wear those garbage bags, Pat," she guffawed. "I'll send pictures back home and blackmail you!"

I snorted at her. "Some things, like survival, are more important than style, Wendy. Maybe you don't know that yet." I was about to continue when I realized everyone we knew at the bar was bent over double. I glared at them and then couldn't help laughing. "You can't judge a book by its cover. I'll go and put on my rain gear."

"Just make sure it's colour coordinated! What goes with orange plastic?" Mac gasped with laughter.

"Wait and see," I threw back as I climbed up to the second floor area.

I returned a few minutes later proudly sporting my orange garbage bag, which didn't entirely cover my bumblebee striped long johns, I was met with derisive comments and laughter.

"How'll you keep it up?" David chortled. "It'll be around your ankles."

"As close as we are, David," I retorted, "there are some things I won't share."

It was getting darker with the storm and nightfall. We walked off to get something to eat, talking and dodging raindrops from opened windows. It won't be an easy day tomorrow, I thought, as I walked into the warmth of the dining room and the fragrance of stew.

It was much later when I crawled into my sleeping bag wearing my long-sleeved t-shirt. I curled up and wrapped the pillow around my shoulders. The cold air worked its way into the folds of the bag. "Psst, you guys! Are you warm enough?" I whispered. "I wish I'd kept my warmer bag."

"Go to sleep," Wendy muttered.

CHAPTER 18

FRIENDSHIP

The early morning light in the dormitory was grey and cold. I stuck my hand out then fell back in the sleeping bag and curled up. Someone went to the window and pulled back the curtains. The dormitory light didn't change and it looked like fog was blanketing the valley.

When I got to the dining room Mac and Wendy were poring over the guidebook and talking to David and Marion.

"So, what's the verdict?" I asked.

"We have a climb of about nine hundred metres and about thirty kilometres of trail," David replied. I sipped my coffee and made no comment. "Not a bad day, eh?"

"Any news on the weather? I see it hasn't gotten any better," I commented.

"You'll have to ask for us," Marion said.

"Guess we'll find out as we walk," I muttered.

The wind came in gusts and I came close again to losing my balance. I stopped for a while and just stood, squinting into the sheets of rain as they sliced down. The tops of the mountain were entirely covered in fog, although from time to time there was a break in the clouds and we could see a small stream of sunlight. We started up the stone trail, trying to avoid the stream coursing down it.

Holding my hood in place I began to walk, placing my feet carefully as I negotiated the steep ridge. It didn't take long till I let the hood fall back, got a desperate grip on my walking stick, and was panting as rain ran down my neck. I had stepped to one side of the trail to catch my breath when I heard the sound of someone striding along. The two Germans marched right past me. "Ja, so good morning," said Helmut over his shoulder. "Safe trip. We see you at the top." I glanced sideways and saw their bare, red feet in sandals, the muddy water running off them.

As I continued walking the clouds began to scuttle across the sky. They lifted just enough that I could see into the valley, which was a sparkling lush green with wild flowers bending graciously in the wind. The fence railings were solid black, faint wisps of steam rising from their rough texture. Just as I thought the fog might lift, it sank again, and I kept on, unable to see anything around me. The rain continued down the stone path in rivulets.

It seemed I'd walked for hours without anyone passing or walking alongside me. I had climbed steadily up the valley and suspected I was near the summit. Suddenly, there was a path to the right. Should I take it, I wondered. I couldn't remember anything about such a path in the guidebook. Would I be able to find my way back here? I looked into the fog; there was nothing to be seen.

"Come on," I chided myself. "You're not going to die here if you make a mistake." Trees appeared and disappeared as the fog moved and shifted. I started to walk to the right and before long I saw a figure in the mist. He stood holding his hat on, his feet planted solidly on the rocky outcropping.

"Hola!" I shouted. He neither moved nor spoke. Puzzled, I took a few steps and realized with a shock that it was a statue of a pilgrim—modern garb for sure, but a statue. Frightened, I turned and got back to the main path. My heart was pounding. Was I losing it, I asked myself as I forged ahead as fast as I could. It was no more than seven hundred metres when I saw the outlines of shops and a building—likely the albergue. Then, as I walked toward the door of one of the shops, I heard a familiar voice, "Pat, come here. These earrings are lovely."

Wendy was standing near a display counter. I glared at her. Why hadn't they waited?

"I'm going inside to have a coffee," I said, and with that I turned on my heel and walked into the albergue where I was met by Mac and the Aussies.

"Hey, Pat," Mac said. "We wondered if you'd make it here or stop in the other albergue."

I stared at him, speechless. Just then Wendy walked in. "I'll get a coffee, too," she smiled. I felt trapped between my relief at seeing them and my anger that they had left me behind. I plunked myself down and started my latte.

When we went up the stairs to our assigned beds, I noticed Helmut and Franz washing their red feet not far from us. Near them sat Geoff repacking his backpack.

The dining bell summoned us to a long log table that held platters of sliced meat cooked medium rare. The first mouthful melted in my mouth. "This is sublime," I said. "What is it? Beef?"

"It's venison," said one of the servers. All I could do was grin.

"It's magnificent," I replied. "I'm Canadian, I should know." Everyone burst into laughter.

We moved away from the dining table to sit in front of the wood fire and sip our brandy. Slowly we climbed up to the dormitory where we saw our assigned single beds—a true luxury after those metal bunks.

• • •

Six o'clock! I could make out the emergency light in the early morning gloom. It cast a red shadow on the wooden siding and outlined the hunched forms in sleeping bags. Several beds away Helmut and Franz were stuffing things into their packs and collecting their laundry, which likely hadn't dried yet. Through the window, I could see the fog and hear the rain beating down on the metal roof. So this was O Cebreiro living up to its reputation.

There was nothing pressing to motivate us, so we had breakfast and left later than usual. The sun was trying desperately to shine through the fog. Leaves glistened in the pale light and water ran along the path, which dropped down through stands of trees, leading us away from the warmth and dryness of the albergue.

Soon we were following the steep path to the valley bottom and walking through fields of flax. As we passed Alto de San Roque, I saw the dramatic statue of a second pilgrim, cloak flying in the wind, one arm stretched forward. Last night when the first figure loomed abruptly out of the mist I had been terrified. Today, looking at this statue pointing to the future, I was reminded of the call of the Camino and how answering that call had affected our lives and our futures.

Our walk continued through the rugged countryside. The weather offered no relief and I was miserably cold. My clothes were again soaking and clung to my legs and back. I had picked up my pace to stay warmer and was walking with Wendy. Suddenly, Mac stopped and called back to us, "There's a bar near the top of this hill. Let's stop for something warm." We walked even more quickly. As Mac held the door open for us we were hit by the smell of dank clothes and bodies. The windows ran with moisture; the floor was wet and dirty. We ordered hot chocolate and took off our wettest clothing. The heat in the room and the rich flavour of the hot chocolate were so welcome. I felt my shoulders relax; my feet began to warm up.

"Time to head out," said Wendy. "We need to keep moving so we get to Triacastela as soon as possible. The rain isn't going to stop. On top of that I'm hungry and there's no food till then." I reluctantly pulled on my rain jacket, tied the hood, and slung the pack on my back. We soldiered on, the glacial rain pelting our faces. Suddenly, I heard the sound of tires on gravel and a grey sedan emerged from the fog, its horn blaring.

"My God," said Mac. "We gotta be on the lookout. I'm sure they can't see us and they'd never be able to stop anyway."

At different times, the senda turned into a tunnel and crossed under the road. Once on the other side it changed back into a muddy track. We slipped and slid down the trail as it wound in and out of the streams of rain. On top of a hill, near the town of Filloval, I caught a rare glimpse of Triacastela in the valley bottom, partially hidden by low fog. As we curved down along the ridge, the sun came out and we saw the beauty of the fields and farms in front of us.

When we neared the city, we began bumping into large numbers of people often walking in small groups. Some walked at an irregular and hurried pace. Others strode along alone, with great purpose. Some carried plastic shopping bags; others had small backpacks. That must be all their gear, I thought in surprise. I turned to three women as they passed me.

"De dónde son ustedes?" I asked.

One of the women turned to me and said, "We're from Madrid. We are walking the last hundred kilometres of the Camino to get the official signature and credencial at the cathedral. This is our third time of doing this. We just love arriving in Santiago—the cathedral, the *botafumeiro* swinging above the altar, clouds of smoke billowing out of it. Everything is so rich in history and colour," she explained. "Don't you just love it?" She looked at me, her eyes bright and inquisitive.

"It's our first Camino," I replied. "We've walked the whole way." I felt superior and at the same time out of step with the world to which we were returning.

She smiled, picked up her pace, and called out to her companions. "She's new. She hasn't done this before." They turned to look at me. We smiled at each other. They turned and walked quickly on. The rain began again in earnest; the morning clouded over and the ragged edge of the cloud moved down the hills.

We arrived some two hours later at the Monasterio de Samos. "Who were the people we met earlier?" I asked the hospitalero who signed us in to the albergue.

"Señora, they are pilgrims, too. If they walk the last hundred kilometres they can get the officially signed credencial. Then they are officially pilgrims—as you are."

I looked at him. "Are you serious? We've walked more than eight hundred kilometres and they get the same standing as us?"

He shrugged eloquently. "That's been the tradition for many generations."

I turned and translated for Wendy and Mac.

"Let's get a coffee, Pat. We're so cold and tired that none of this makes sense," said Mac.

"Bloody hell," I muttered to myself as I glanced into the albergue. The frames of the bunks were rusty and the mattress gave off the dank smell of mould. "This isn't much of a place. We could have walked on to Sarria," I complained.

There was a long silence. "I think we should see if we can take in the high mass," said Wendy. "It might increase our feelings of charity." Mac was the first to laugh, then Wendy joined in. I grinned.

"Nothing like a laugh to warm us up," I added. We made our bunks, left our packs on them, and headed for the cathedral.

We walked in just as the monks, chanting mass, entered through a door by the altar. There were eight of them, hands in their sleeves, heads bowed. Their voices floated up through the high arches. I felt my shoulders relax as I waited for the familiar mass to fill my world. It took a few minutes to realize that the sound that I had so anticipated was actually rather thin and it quavered slightly. It lacked the deep warmth of male voices. I looked more closely and saw the white hair, stooped shoulders, and the slight tremor of the conductor's hands as he set the pace for the timing, then took his place.

We walked out together, silent. "What did you think?" Wendy asked, looking at Mac and me.

I waited a while before answering. "The sung mass is suffering from the old men and their voices. They are likely putting everything into it, but the result is painful. And the future is not promising. There are so few novitiates in the church. Remember the other mass? Only three singers. It feels as though they've given up trying to keep the music alive. It makes me want to protest. We are letting this disappear without a fight."

We walked back to the albergue. There were few pilgrims in the dormitory and the room was freezing. I undressed and crawled into my damp sleeping bag. As the heat from my body spread, I took out my diary to begin writing. I thumbed through a few pages and noted with regret how little I had written. How would I remember so many events, conversations, moments of beauty? A little late to think of that, I chastised myself. At the same time I felt instinctively that the memories would stay with me forever.

Sleep ran its hand along my back. It was time to rest and be ready for tomorrow's long walk. I hoped with all my heart that the rain would stop.

The next morning I woke up before the alarm, gasping for air. My makeshift pillow was against my face, the smell of mould overwhelming. I turned and twisted in my sleeping bag, dressing inside it for warmth. I had slept with all my clothes in the bag. Unfortunately, the strategy had not worked. My socks were still damp and so were my pants.

There was no smell of coffee as we walked by the kitchen. The lights were off and no one was about. Wendy had apples she shared and I had some very hard, dry cheese. We walked quickly in the spitting rain looking for the lights of a café. When we finally got to a small restaurant I saw our shadows in its windows. The hoods were pulled down low and rain ran down our jackets.

"My God," I said. "We look so miserable."

Our pace was much slower than the day before. Within an hour we had spread out in our usual pattern. There was no pleasure in the rainy landscape nor in the occasional pilgrim we encountered.

Lunchtime came and went. The clouds rolled back; the rain and wind stopped. The sun's heat grew stronger, leaning its weight on my pack. It was three o'clock when I realized that I was tired. Tired physically, emotionally, and spiritually. I wanted to be in a hotel—comfortable, no pack on my back, a glass of ruby red wine in my hand. It was then that I saw Wendy and Mac. They were leaning over a table in front of a small bar, examining a map.

"How goes it?" I called out. Wendy looked weary.

"It's my pack again," she said. "It just isn't sitting right. Mac has taken over a lot of my things."

"It's nothing," he said as he looked at me appraisingly. "Looks to me that we all need a place to stay, right?" I nodded, mute.

"There's a hotel not far from here—or at least that's what the guidebook says." We clustered around him, looking at the map and working out how to get there.

"Likely about twenty minutes of walking—if we don't get lost," I said. "Let's take a cab."

Mac shook his head. "Not much farther, Pat, we can hoof it."

We set off slowly. The traffic was heavy, the rusty smell of exhaust strong. The first hotel was boarded up, an invitation to the graffiti sprawled on its walls. I asked the café waiter if there was another hotel nearby. He shook his head. We headed off in search of another choice. My feet ached all the way up to my knees. The pack got heavier with each step. Wendy and Mac were quiet. We crossed a major thoroughfare to a kiosk to ask for directions again. The Spaniard's directions were rapid fire and I had trouble translating for Mac, who was plotting our way on the map. They crossed the street, but I stayed on the other side. Tears of fatigue were welling up in my eyes.

"Come on over, Pat," shouted Wendy. "We can see it from here. It's behind that tall building."

I kept walking on my side. The thought of stepping down off the curb hurt in advance. Finally, we found ourselves in front of a hotel of the sixties. Its faded glory reflected how I felt. The carpets were a bit tattered, the colours old and dark, the receptionist's shirt was soiled. We took the elevator up to the sixth floor. No one talked. Mac and Wendy opened their door. My key turned easily in the lock and I collapsed on the bed. The pain surged up from my feet.

"Jesus," I thought. "Jesus. I don't want to go to dinner." I slowly hauled myself to the shower. The stream of brownish warm water felt divine. I washed my hair, the shampoo running into my eyes. As I dried off with a towel that had done many years of service, I started to feel human again. A twinge of guilt ran through me. Why had I refused to cross the street and walk with them? I thought of how it must have looked to Mac and Wendy. Well, a glass of beer will change everything, I thought. There was a knock at my door.

"Let's go to McDonald's," said Wendy. We all laughed.

"I never go back home—but heck, this may make it feel like home," I said. We headed out to the restaurant with the golden arches. The waiter came up and asked for our order. "Three quarter pounders with cheese," said Mac.

"They taste like sawdust," said Wendy, her mouth twisted. We chewed silently. My weariness returned.

"Let's go into the centre and see the sights," said Mac with enthusiasm. My energy sank a notch lower. "Tell you what," I said. "I'll have a snooze. I'm really tired. And we'll get together for supper." I headed back to the hotel and fell instantly into a deep sleep. My dreams were dark and full of foreboding. I woke up with my mouth dry; my eyes felt like sandpaper. I was rinsing my face when they knocked.

"Greetings, pilgrims," I said with false bravado. "Where shall we eat? Did you see any exciting places?"

"Well," said Mac, "had we only known, just two blocks west there are some really nice modern hotels and a few restaurants. But, of course, who's to know when you're a newcomer."

We headed off to the elevator and went into the hotel bar. It was decorated in deep reds, dark wood, and smelled of years of use. A small group of Spaniards sat together in a corner.

"Must be from the conference advertised in the lobby," said Wendy. "Those women are really nicely dressed." The two women at the table were in animated conversation with the men. We sat down near them. One looked over at us and smiled.

"Where are you from?" she asked.

"Canada," I replied.

"José," she called out to one of the men. "These people are from Canada."

"Come sit over here," José gestured. "We're going to meet in Montreal next year." It was much later when Mac said he thought it was time to go and eat. My stomach curled at the idea.

"You go ahead, Mac," I said. "I'll take it easy tonight." A sense of desolation rose in me. I tried to smile. "You guys go," I said again. "I'm going to take a bit of a break."

"Are you okay, Pat?" Wendy asked, her eyes showing concern. "You've never taken a break in the evening before."

"Yes, yes. I'm fine, truly. It was a long day."

I got back to my room and lay down. The bed felt foreign; I could tell the lumps and bumps would bother me all night long. The desire to cry was overwhelming. Just then, there was a knock at the door. I wiped my eyes and said, "Yes?"

"It's us," Wendy said.

I opened the door to see them standing with a bottle of wine in one hand, a barbecued chicken in a plastic dish in the other, and a baguette.

"You guys …" I started.

"It's a picnic," said Wendy. "We remembered our first night in St. Jean-Pied-de-Port and thought it was time for another."

"Come on in," I said, my smile a little crooked. "It's good …"

"Yep," said Mac, "I even found a bottle opener." He gave a pull and the "thunk" of the cork filled the room.

"Come over here," I said. "Have we got enough glasses? We can use our towels for a picnic table. Hey, this is great!"

A sense of gratitude welled up in me. Would I have continued tomorrow morning without this time together? I wasn't sure. In the meantime, the smell of chicken, the sight of the wine, and the feeling of togetherness was more than enough.

CHAPTER 19

HE DIES SLOWLY
WHO DOES
NOT TRAVEL

When I woke, I was curled up in a ball clutching the threadbare blanket wrapped around my shoulders. The room was dark and I could just make out the solid form of the chest of drawers against the white walls. A thin shaft of light from the street shone through the French doors, which didn't shut tightly. I was settling down for a few more moments of sleep just as the high-pitched rat-tat of the alarm clock broke the silence. I wiggled my toes, stretched and yawned, then stood up on the cold, hard wooden floor. The miracle had happened again. I rocked back and forth on my feet. No pain! How did that happen? Yesterday, it seemed that the pain was in every corner of my being—and today, voilà!

No point in dwelling on it, I thought. Might tempt the devil. I splashed warm water on my face, pulled on my clothes, and began stuffing things into my backpack.

I was pulling my door shut just as Mac and Wendy stepped into the thin light of the hallway.

"Morning," whispered Wendy. "How'd you sleep? We nearly froze."

"Me, too," I replied. None of us mentioned yesterday. We continued down the stairs without talking. The reception area was in darkness,

although I could make out the sleeping form of the night watchman. The
city was waking up to the hum of traffic and the growl of big trucks. Lights
were on in buildings and apartment blocks. It's autumn, I reminded myself.
The day begins for some of us and then the sun rises.

We walked back past the golden arches of McDonald's. Even in the
darkness it looked so familiar. We could be on any street in Canada. Our
boots echoed hollowly between the buildings as we followed the arrows
to the main highway. Headlights of cars, the throb of their engines, and
the whoosh as they passed us was unreal. Suddenly, out of the darkness a
huge transport bore down on us. The small lights on top of the cab and the
gleam of the radiator grill were like a science fiction beast. I made out the
pale face of the driver as he passed, his eyes intent on the road in front of
him. We came to a traffic circle, waited for a momentary break in the traffic,
and moved in unison. I felt the rhythm of my walking quicken. Ahead of
me, Wendy and Mac were talking quietly.

As I passed darkened windows I could make out the outline of
machine parts, advertisements for tools, the tops of counters and
computers. The weeds were high along the sidewalk. Pilgrims walking
by had likely broken down some of the thistles. I suddenly heard the
"vroom" of a motorbike and jumped quickly to avoid being hit. My heart
was pounding. That was close. Just imagine, nearly finished walking the
Camino only to be run over by a motorcycle.

Stefan's death had happened like that early one morning in a violent,
unforeseeable moment. He died at an unmarked railway crossing while
driving to work. It was so long ago and yet my heart wrenched at the
memory. I had been twenty years old and living the phase of my life that
the French call "l'amour des vingt ans," the love of twenty year olds, the
first love, sensual and compelling.

I remembered knowing how much he wanted me. The night before his
death we had had a lovers' quarrel: the petty sort that happens in first loves.
I knew how much power I wielded. I decided not to see him that evening;
he could just wait, suffer a little. He called back. Still I said no. Untouched
by the years, the guilt of his death lay inside me.

The sunrise touched the road in front of us and the white lines stood out from the blackened concrete. Some cars had dimmed their headlights. The haze was lifting from the pavement in wisps. We could see clearly the outline of a roof in a nearby farmyard.

"It's over here," called Wendy, her walking stick waving in the air. "Thank God, we're leaving this noisy freeway."

The path was rocky and wet in places. We started down the steep slope of trees that outlined the front of the house. Cows had their heads in the deep grass and we heard the occasional tone of their bells, mournful in the hush of early morning.

His death had happened just before Easter. Months later, on my way to work, I saw the dilemmas of life. They stretched out before me with clarity. Love, death, luck can all happen in an instant. They don't take years to occur; they can't be readily controlled or produced. They just happen because we are alive. That's all it takes.

That day many years ago, I understood the inevitability of death. We don't seek it out, but we can't avoid it. Our strength lies in how we spend the hours that we call "life," how we spend the commodity called "time." Our possessions. Our resources. I vowed there would be no lingering guilt or fear the next time I encountered death. Somehow, I would find a touchstone—something that would be a reminder for me on any day, at any moment. Like beauty, which seems to be beyond time and place, in all contexts and surroundings. I knew that in loving others I wanted to close each day with forgiveness. I wanted to be with people I loved without controlling or being controlled.

Suddenly, I slipped on the gravel and slid over a flat rock. As I lost my balance I fell backward, sitting down abruptly. I got up and brushed off my hands and shorts. My heart was pounding. That was a close one.

I slowed down and kept an eye on the loose gravel spread unevenly over the flat rocks. Well, I thought, those guiding principles are still with me. And in the shadows so is the haunting knowledge—and fear—that each moment is pivotal, has its own potential and its own risk.

I walked on, watching how the sun woke up the landscape, warmed my back, and lifted the morning breezes. The morning noises grew louder. The sound of voices in the fields, the cows lowing. Everything beckoned me to turn inward, to hold and savour the sights, sounds, and smells of the land.

I thought idly of Coelho's guide and decided to summon him. Suddenly, I stopped walking. The guide's eyes! My God! They were Stefan's eyes: soft, brown, wise beyond their years. The message that I am where I should be … that too felt like him. The sense of being loved, accepted … I shook my head. It's a mirage. I'm making connections where there are none. Or am I? Isn't this like Mac's old man—himself at eighty years of age? Doesn't reality just twist and turn at times? And doesn't it feel like the truth? Like a reality waiting for you?

I wanted to catch up with Wendy and Mac. I needed some sense of everyday reality. At the outskirts of the next dun-brown village stood a modern sign: "Internet—beside the church." I quickened my step. Maybe some email messages would cut off the questions, the doubts, and the haunting sense of the worlds within my reach. Worlds I could touch, live in—if I had the resources, the strength.

The light of the computer screens outlined the profiles and hunched backs of other pilgrims. I typed in my password and watched as the inbox came up. The first message was from Brian. We had known each other since undergraduate days when we wrestled with French and Spanish irregular verbs. He had attached a poem by Martha Medeiros. The first line of the poem pierced my being. It began: "Il meurt lentement celui qui ne voyage pas …" and finished with "Vis aujourd'hui!" "He dies slowly who does not travel … Live for today!" It felt as though someone had been listening and watching my day.

Strangely comforted by the poem, I signed off the Internet and headed back out into the heat of the day. We had so little time left to walk, to be on this Camino.

The demanding rains of Galicia had stopped. It was a gentle, loving sky: wisps of clouds, soft blues, and infinite space—like the sky in a Fragonard painting I first saw in France. Since then I've seen those skies in Canada, and now in Spain. I'll tell Brian about this, I thought.

The path continued along a ridge and then dropped down into farmland where cattle stood grazing. Sheep were lying in a nearby field burned brown by the heat. I glanced around casually. No shepherd in sight.

As I walked past, a dog threw himself on the gate. His head was huge; his jowls were pulled back. I was taken aback by the sight of his maw, the white of his teeth. He lunged again and his front paws dug into the mesh of the gate. I jumped back in alarm. He was immense, black and brown. A Rottweiler cross of some sort. I watched in horror as each lunge grew more vicious than the last. I started to run, knowing it was useless. Headlines of dog attacks flashed in my mind. I looked over my shoulder and saw him moving back toward the sheep. His walk was stiff legged and deliberate. My heart rate began to slow. I had heard stories of rabid dogs in Spain. They are considered one of the hazards of the Camino. Up till now we had been so lucky—no dogs on the loose. Perhaps because we were closer to Santiago and these towns saw more tourists.

That night the albergue we found was huge. There were sixty bunks per room. The bathrooms had no soap, no shower curtains, and no toilet paper.

"Thus ends the first and final chapter of my sojourn in albergues," I said to Wendy and Mac as we set off in search of a restaurant. The street was full of pilgrims, shouting, laughing, and dancing past us. Some waved bottles of beer. We found a quiet corner in a small restaurant just as Franz and Helmut walked in. Their red faces beamed good will. As they sat down, Helmut said, "Well, it looks like we'll make it, ja?"

Mac said, "Yes," and we all nodded in agreement. I felt again my sense of reluctance. I didn't want it to end. Don't do it. Just stay walking. Just stay in the moment. I smiled ironically.

"So what's the joke?" asked Franz. "You look amused." They turned to me, quizzically.

"I don't want to stop walking this Camino," I blurted out. "I want to just keep doing what we've been doing: walking, meeting people, being in Spain."

"That's not sensible," said Mac. "We've planned to finish and we are going to do it in spite of the many challenges. This is one hell of an achievement, Pat. You know that."

"Yeah, I do. You're right. But I have come to love this time, the immediacy, the sense of purpose ..."

"Ja, well, my purpose is to go home, now," said Franz. "Home to

Düsseldorf, to my own bed and my own house. No more walking."

Dinner arrived and silence fell. I knew that I could not stop time. Indeed, I had just spent more than thirty days learning to live in the moment. I knew what happened to me when I projected ahead or analyzed the past. Nothing could stop the pleasure of living in the moment, right here, right now. The night air was cold as we walked back.

The dormitory was full of people and sounded like the Tower of Babel. At nine-thirty someone shut off the lights. I closed my diary and pulled the sleeping bag close to my face. The calm of sleep slowly enveloped my body.

Somewhere during the night I awoke. The noises around me were terrifying. Where was I? Surely this is a dream, I thought. I lay still, listening. The noises were human not animal. Every tone of snoring, snorting, trumpeting, farting, and calling out could be heard from my bedmates that night. I grimaced. This is the last albergue of my life, I thought as I rolled over.

Dawn came early. The room was full of agitated movement as people dressed, packed, and headed off without looking around or talking to one other. I looked across the bunks to see Franz sitting bolt upright, face red and scowling. "That is the last time I stay here, in an albergue, ja!" he exclaimed, his accent heavier than usual. "I did not sleep with the noises. And someone shut the window. This was not pleasant."

By lunch, the rain had turned into a drizzle. The restaurant was packed when I walked in. Wendy and Mac were nowhere to be seen and I understood why: Portomarín was too far away to waste time in a restaurant. I grabbed a large sandwich and found a table. I finished my coffee and walked out into a grey landscape, but no rain. My spirits soared. Perhaps we had at last found the end of Galicia's cold, rainy weather.

"Patricia!" I heard my name called as I was crossing an open soccer field. I turned and saw Hélène talking with a small group.

"Hello there! Great to see you!" I called back. We hugged.

"I thought I might never see you again," she said. "How perfect! Now we can walk together."

I hid my disappointment. Walking and meditating had become my morning ritual and I didn't want company, not even Hélène's. She was wearing a narrow brimmed hat. Her eyes shone and her skin glowed with health. Like me she had lost a lot of weight and her body looked reconfigured. We fell into a natural rhythm. Easy, like old friends.

"So," I began. "Tell me what it has been like for you? The visit with the priest at the monastery was good?"

She was looking straight ahead. "It was an eye opener—is that how you say it? I never went to church much. I am a child of the sixties and I have so many questions as I walk this Camino. I asked him many things, like good and evil—where do they come from? What does death mean? Is there such a place as heaven? As hell? For me, the Camino is a religious experience. But he had no answers. This will find its way into one of my art works. I don't know for sure how, but I know it will be there. You know how it is. The colour and line form a place for emptiness in paintings. It will be that subtle."

I looked at her quizzically. "These questions trouble you?"

We stopped. She looked at me. "That is the word—trouble. Yes, they do. But I find no answers. Perhaps I just live with them. Just make them into irritating companions of the voyage. I will keep on bumping into them, I know." She grinned at me. "A bit like you, Patricia. You also I keep bumping into."

We started to walk again. I paused then decided to talk with her about my quest. "I don't have those questions, you know, Hélène. But I have had such an experience in these days of walking. The more I walk the more I feel united, profoundly united, in my being. My body, my soul, my mind, my feelings, they are inextricably interwoven. I have always talked about this, but now I actually feel it and live it. I am troubled, like you, with how to live with this new reality once I am back in Canada—in my everyday world. I have experienced such joy, such peace and groundedness. I don't know where it comes from, what world it is. It feels like the air and the wind are embodiments of these ideas. So easy to feel, yet so hard to put a finger on. So difficult to dress up with words so that others can see them. I feel terrified in some ways, emboldened in others. You know, it is new, this feeling of being whole, and at the same time the structure of the ideas is as old as anything I can remember in my life."

She looked at me intently. "Tell me more. I am not sure I can follow you.

Is this some sort of image? Music? Form? How do you know it is there?"

"It's in the pace I walk, which is the essential pace on the path of my life; a path that I am beginning to know and understand. It is an organic thing. My walking and meditating shape it. As I walk, it grows in me, from the ground up."

I looked at her over my shoulder. I felt somewhat embarrassed and ill at ease. "I likely sound a bit off. One of my cousins told me that my emails sounded odd. He wants to know if I am becoming Catholic." We both laughed in relief. "Well," I said. "Let's stop for a coffee in the next town. I think the rain will hit before we make it there."

The sky had darkened, the wind had picked up, and the leaves were scuttling along the path. We quickened our pace just as the first raindrops hit. They pelted down. We ran for cover in a nearby underpass and turned to watch. The rain sluiced down; trees were bent with the gale. Water ran down our faces. We shivered in the cold, dark space of the overpass.

"We need to get to a warm place, Hélène," I said. She nodded mutely. We had both pulled on extra clothes but were soaked to the skin and shivering. Thunder rumbled ominously. We heard shouting and soon two men ran up. "Bloody well freezing," one of them said in a strong Scottish accent. "Want some tea, luv?"

I nodded mutely. The steam rose from the thermos; he poured the strong tea into my cup.

"We're going to make a run for it," said the tall Scot.

"Really?" said Hélène. "It'll be a long run, a bit too much in this rain. I think we'll just sit it out."

"Right!" said the Scot. "We're off. Hope you ladies make it before nightfall."

We sat down against the stone wall. I rummaged in my pack and found some apples, almonds, and dark chocolate, and Hélène discovered some dried-up cheese.

"Time for a picnic," she announced. "This is just like Plato's cave, isn't it? There are no shadows on the wall, but with a little imagination it could be the ideal world as he saw it. Just shadows dancing on the walls."

We both laughed. It was then that I realized we were tense. We were caught between our talk, the storm, and the cold. We were uncomfortable with sitting still, with the sound of the rain, and the dampness of our shelter. The easy rhythm of the pace, of the movement was suspended. I wrapped my arms around my bare, cold legs and rested my head on my arms. I could feel the warmth begin to penetrate my body. A comfortable silence sat with us then slowly unravelled as we heard the rain let up.

"Shall we give it a go?" I asked, standing up and brushing off my shorts. "I don't really like this shelter—it's colder than if we were moving. How's about it? Ready to go outside?"

"I think it's ominous," said Hélène. "It is as though we are cut off from the Camino. We have just stepped a little way from it, but it feels—how do you say... 'sombre'—dark, and it makes me worry. I don't even know about what. So yes, let's get going." She bent over her pack and put in the last of the cheese and my almonds.

As we left the underpass, the wind hit us. It went through my Gore-Tex and I could feel the goosebumps rise. My hood flapped against my pack. The landscape was the dull yellow of burnt grass, wet dun-coloured clay, and dark trees. They swayed in the wind. I could hear the flap of Hélène's jacket. Half-walking, half-running, we found the senda. There were other pilgrims also bent against the wind. The sight of Arca welcomed us. Soon we'd be warm.

As we walked past some restaurants I looked for Wendy and Mac. "Look, Hélène," I said, "you stay in this restaurant and I'll ask for them down the main street. I'll get us a room at the hotel and then I'll come back." Just as I was heading for the hotel, Wendy and Mac walked in.

"Where were you?" I asked, irritated. "I've looked everywhere."

Their eyes shifted. "Just up the hill. There's a little hotel there. We came back looking for you." My irritation vanished. I was so cold.

"Well, let's have dinner after you've warmed up a bit," said Mac. "You go and find a hotel room. Then we'll meet here. David and Marion got into the albergue. How long do you need? The menu looks okay." Outside there was a faint rumble of thunder.

It was much later when Hélène and I returned to the restaurant. We had taken the time to shower and find clothes that weren't soaked. We walked in and I pushed back my hood. My hands were bright red from the cold. Outside, the rain streaked down the windows. Inside, they were covered with steam. Branches formed shadows, tapped nervously, then disappeared briefly only to attack again. The gale howled. Inside, we were wrapped up in steam and the rich smell of food. I heard laughing and looked over to see Mac, Wendy, and the Aussies. There was already an empty bottle of red wine on the table and Mac was finishing off a glass. Hélène and I shook off our jackets and walked over, rain dripping off us. We arrived in a puddle at the table.

"You are celebrating a day early," said Hélène. "We have one more day of walking to go."

Their cheeks glowed with happiness and good food. "We're going to keep on going toward Santiago," Wendy declared. Her eyes sparkled. "I want to be there tonight. I'm ready to be received into the order. I want my final credencial now."

Mac put his arm around her. "We've done twenty-eight clicks today. Isn't that enough for you, you woman of passion? How's about a little patience?"

Wendy looked deeply into his eyes. "Nope, I'm going on. Come with me." It was more of a command than an invitation.

Mac grinned down at her. "Nothing stops this woman," he said to us. "Nothing. So let's hit the road." They stood up. Wendy put a bill on the table. "This will cover our meal and the tip," she said, turning quickly to Mac.

I stood wordless. She looked over at me. "We'll be in Santiago at the exact moment when the botafumeiro swings for the first time tomorrow. Can't you just imagine that huge, smoking chandelier? Won't it be amazing? Isn't it great we'll be able to make it?"

I nodded. I heard the breath escape from my lungs. "We booked a hotel for the next night in Santiago …" I started feebly.

"Don't worry. We'll make sure they keep it for you," Mac threw over his shoulder as he opened the door. The wind barged into the dining room, blowing in dead leaves and puddles of rain on the floor. The cold invaded, forced out the warmth. The venetian blinds rattled fretfully. The door slammed shut. No one spoke. The storm continued, the branches slashing the window. David and Marion looked at us.

"Sit down, there's a little bit left," Marion said. "If you don't want it, I'll finish it off."

I set my pack on the floor, wiped my face on my sleeve, and sat down. I felt my shoulders slump. I couldn't move. I watched as Hélène went up to the till. She scanned the menu behind the waitress and gave her order. She stood on one foot, waiting for the change. I heard the chef in the kitchen call out the order as he snapped the chit above the window opening.

I sat for a minute, listening to the voices, to the sound of the branches on the window, to David who was telling the story of his day. I smiled at him, having heard nothing. I got up then. The till was only a few steps away and I heard the slap of my wet boots as I walked over the tiled floor to place my order.

Why hadn't they talked to me about the decision? Didn't they want me with them? How could that be true? They looked so totally absorbed in each other. I replayed the scene. So much laughter, such pleasure evidenced in the empty bottles of wine on the table. Had they talked over the decision? Somehow, I knew they hadn't.

The chef called out an order and Hélène jumped up, heading for the open window.

I nodded to David, who continued to regale me with his story of the day's walk.

The chef called out again, looking at me across the dining room. I made my way to the window and ordered a bottle of red wine. The wine was rough, up front, and personal. I coughed and choked on the first mouthful. Marion leaned over and slapped me on the back. I gagged a bit more, tears streaming down my face.

"Hey, don't take it so seriously," said Hélène sitting opposite me, eating her soup. "If you just take a little sip … " She picked up her glass and demonstrated. Her eyes twinkled over the edge of the glass. "See. I don't gag."

Still coughing, I wiped my eyes and nodded. David and Marion got up and started up the stairs, saying, "See you early. Let's head off by seven as usual—together," David called over his shoulder.

"Well," said Hélène, "it's been a long day and a cold one." Her

Quebecois accent was strong, a sign of fatigue. I switched to French for her. We chatted about the day, the weather, about getting to Santiago. As far as I could tell, their departure had no impact on her. She didn't see anything unusual in it. I didn't bring it up.

The storm raged unabated. I sat there, looking out the window. I found myself wondering about them. Would they get cold? Wet? Tired from the storm? I could see them in my mind's eye walking along the path, dodging puddles as we had done all week long. I was glad to be in the steamy interior with the strong smells of Spanish cooking.

I ordered another bottle of wine. Our talk was easy, full of reminiscences of our Camino, our homes. I thought how Canadian we were in spite of language, of home base. We shared something unique. And we were women: she with children, me with none; her marriage still intact but bent and worn; my own, long since gone.

Our room was small with twin beds and a bathroom. I lay in bed listening to the sound of the shower as I waited to turn out the lights. It struck me that this part of my life was nearly finished. What would it feel like to arrive in the square in front of the cathedral? I looked at my pack, the scallop shell still attached to the strap along with the miniature Virgin Mary medallion.

The next morning I woke early just as Hélène came out of the bathroom. She was wrapped in a towel: her hair was dripping. "I will walk into Santiago alone. We are like soulmates. If I walk with you, I will lose some of why I set off on my own, why I left Bernard behind."

I stared at her.

"You understand, don't you? It has to be my experience. Mine alone." She began towelling her hair.

"This is t-to-too early for such serious conversations," I said, stuttering. "I'm not awake yet. But, hey, sure, if you want to walk alone I would not stand in your way. Just give me a minute to adjust to being awake, okay?"

"It is not against you, Patricia," she said. "But we are so alike—you know that." It sounded as though she had said "dat." She said it looking at me from across the room. "This means we share too much for the ending to be for me."

I looked at her closely. Her face was tense, her eyes focused on me, on my eyes. Her expression portrayed concern—and determination.

"We'll see each other in Santiago and talk about it, all right?" She nodded. I nodded.

Outside the storm had stopped, but the room was still chilly and damp. I sat alone in the restaurant. Just like the first day. I thought about yesterday and the dank air of the culvert under the overpass. Nothing had been the same after that. I set off a little before seven, with David and Marion. Hélène had already left—on her own—sometime after breakfast.

The sun was shining. David and Marion were moving along quickly. They had decided to visit Lavacolla, where pilgrims had traditionally bathed before going into Santiago.

"Are you going to run the five kilometres to Monte del Gozo, too?" I asked.

"Not on your life," laughed David. "My feet are finally cured and I don't want to encourage problems. See you in Santiago." We hugged and they turned off.

I followed the signs. In my mind there was a thunderous silence. My heart was numb, empty. The crowds of people passing by were so gay. Their laughter filled my emptiness. Just over my shoulder I heard "Buen Camino." I looked back and saw a clean-cut American man walking near a group but on his own. He came over to me, said nothing, and put himself in my pace. We walked like that, quietly, for more than an hour. When I looked over at his group, I realized they were turning off the senda and heading to a café.

"So long," he said, shaking my hand as he turned to follow the group. "I've enjoyed walking with you." I smiled and kept walking, aware of the heat, of the noise of other pilgrims as they celebrated the closing kilometres. I wanted to stop all the noises behind me for the last kilometres. They started singing, "We all live in a yellow submarine, a yellow submarine." The repetition and the noise grated on me. But, as I walked on, my usual sense of rhythm returned and I changed my pace to walk with it. I began to hum along with the singing. I found myself smiling as I passed other pilgrims.

Suddenly, I was in Santiago. It was the last few minutes of the Camino. I was walking by myself along the narrow stone street to the Oficina del

Pelegrino south of the cathedral. I entered and stood in the lineup to receive my documents of the pilgrimage. I was numb with anticipation and fear. In front of me, women were in tears. Men were standing stunned. Other groups were laughing hysterically. I finally found myself standing at the counter.

"What is your status?" asked the young Spanish woman behind the counter. "How far did you walk?" Her glance took me in softly and warmly.

"I walked 810 kilometres," I said. She smiled, asking for my name. I couldn't speak, so mutely I handed her my credencial.

"Patricia," she said, repeating my name. "That is a beautiful name."

I nodded, the tears on my cheeks. I walked out of the office, past the lineups, seeking a quieter place and found myself behind the cathedral, in a plaza made of Roman tiles. In the centre I could make out a brass plaque about sixty centimetres in diameter. A group of women was standing there, each with a foot on the edge of the plaque. Another woman stood focusing a camera. They were laughing loudly. They're a little hysterical, I thought. When they saw me watching them, they called me over.

"Look over here," said one of them. She pointed to the plaque, which had "0 km" deeply engraved on it. They gestured for my camera and offered to take my picture.

"Una sonrisa," said their guide. I gave her a smile.

I still couldn't talk, but suddenly, as I stood in the plaza before the cathedral surrounded by all the other pilgrims, I saw the depth of what had happened to me: how integrated my life—my mind, heart, body, and soul—had become; how Wendy and Mac were a part of all that had happened to me. The vision was intense. I saw the Camino, the journey, and all its steps. It was like a patchwork quilt. I saw deep inside myself, marvelled at what I had learned, marvelled at what we had said "yes" to and completed. I struck off toward the hotel where my friends and I had agreed to meet. I walked alone but was surrounded by other pilgrims. We laughed, we cried, we hugged each other. My pace was easy, the pack a comfort. I wanted never to stop. I wanted to walk forever.

EPILOGUE

We shall not cease from exploration, and the end of all our exploring will be to arrive where we started and know the place for the first time.

– T. S. Eliot

The plaza in front of the cathedral was bathed in the warm rays of the afternoon sun. Sounds of voices, laughter, and elation filled it, overflowing into the small narrow side streets. Conversations erupted spontaneously. No need to know each other's names, or places—we had a bond. We had walked the "Way," the Camino. The ancient Chinese believed that an invisible, unbreakable thread connects all those who are destined to be together.

I headed off to meet Mac and Wendy at the hotel as we had agreed. As I walked I became aware that we had a rhythm, established unconsciously by following a set daily pattern. Each morning we started off together with the call of the Way. We came together again at the close of the day to talk, to find community. I didn't want to go into the cathedral without them. Suddenly, I saw them walking across the cathedral steps and called out their names. They turned, looked over their shoulders, and their faces lit up with smiles. We met in the middle, arms outstretched, laughing with emotion.

"By God," Mac said, "we did it! We actually did it."

I nodded, my arm around Wendy's shoulder, tears streaming down our cheeks. We hugged each other, holding on hard, slapped each other on the back for loss for words.

"Now we can visit the cathedral together," I said excitedly

"Let's give it a miss," said Wendy. "We can go in the morning to the pilgrims' mass and see the botafumeiro. Let's have a beer now. It's time to celebrate!"

We turned toward the sound of voices coming from a tavern that looked onto the plaza. The sun streamed in through a large dusty window highlighting the faces and profiles of so many we knew.

"Eh, bien," Patrick said. "Le hasard fait si bien les choses. Voilà les *Canacks*!"

The conversation was charged with energy. We reminisced, ordered more beer, made promises to stay in touch. The air was heady with people talking over one another, with laughter, with jokes.

Suddenly, there was a lull in the talk. Geoff looked me in the eye. "What we all want to know is how did you stay friends, you three?"

I looked at Mac and Wendy. "Well," I said, "it's like this. We grew closer apart." The silence was intense.

"So, that's your answer?" Franz asked.

"Yes," I replied. "And remember, you taught me, Franz, that what happens on the Camino stays on the Camino."

The voices began to crescendo; laughter erupted. I looked at Mac and Wendy and we smiled at each other. No matter what, it was our Camino.

The early evening air was cool, almost cold when we left. The plaza was still full of celebration. People called out to each other, dancing and running along the darkened streets. It was then that I saw a familiar solitary figure. "Hélène," I shouted. "Viens donc! We're going for a cognac!"

She turned, her face caught in the glow of the last rays of the sunset. Our eyes locked. I raised my hand to beckon to her. She turned and continued walking. I knew then with a certainty that sent a chill through me that I would never see her again.

"That's odd," Mac said. "Wasn't that Hélène?" I nodded, looked back, but she was gone.

• • •

The next year was a challenge. On the global scene the tragedy of the Japan tsunami and its aftermath shook the world. The EU had a profound crisis as it aimed to integrate its members more closely. Alongside of this, the Canadian government alerted its public to a possible deficit in the pension funds. On the local front, four Royal Canadian Mounted Police were killed in the line of duty. Much of what had seemed stable was under attack and vulnerable.

At the end of October, I left the Camino alive with the sense of an inner world that was deeply and seamlessly integrated. I often repeated my chant to myself: body-mind-spirit-heart. In those moments, an expansiveness, a vibrancy filled my body with joy and a sense of being.

I arrived in Canada before Christmas with a commitment to live my new-found spirituality. After the holidays I planned to rework my writings, workshops, and speeches using that perspective. This proved difficult. Spirituality, I discovered, was not easily massaged. Family, friends, and colleagues listened patiently to my excited accounts of my inner journey— then talked about hockey and February escapes far from the Canadian winter.

The feelings of loneliness and confusion were all too familiar. The Camino experiences had changed me. I intended to live differently, to be fully present in the world whose familiarity now began to stifle me. I wanted to design new strategies, new approaches better suited to my new values. I hesitated—some days bold, others shivering with anxiety, confusion, and—yes—fear.

It could have been a backdrop for a cold dark day in Galicia. The rain was icy and invasive. My path was obscured; there was no way forward. I could not find the cheery yellow flechas, my guides. The beginning, which had seemed full of promise, was as fleeting as the image of my father, or as bleak as the empty space Hélène had left behind.

What was the truth? Had I only imagined this bright promise of a new way to proceed? Could I call it back?

Months passed. The "old strategies" still worked. Why fret? After all, I convinced myself, reworking my business wasn't really necessary, not terribly important. And yet … how would it be to live with my back to this fragile, new identity?

It happened one day the following summer on a mountaintop in Switzerland looking down hundreds of metres at the tiny hamlet of Grunewald. With a clarity that left me speechless, I saw myself at a crossroads. I knew I was in less danger descending this four-thousand-metre peak than I would be if I said "no" to the path, unmarked and uncharted, that lay before me. Like Luther when he tacked his articles of faith on the church door, I had to embrace my beliefs. I could no longer sidestep the commitment to go ahead.

It felt so familiar, this leap of faith. Then, our first night in St. Jean-Pied-de-Port came back. I heard again the tentativeness in my voice, "I'm not fully resident in my life." It was true again. The circle was complete.

Snow-covered mountaintops stretched along the endless horizon against a startlingly blue sky. Their beauty moved me to tears as I did up my harness, attached the carabiners, and faced the challenge before me.

ACKNOWLEDGEMENTS

I owe a debt of gratitude to:

- My constant companions on the Camino: Wendy and Mac. A special thank you to Wendy for crafting the Foreword of this book.

- David and Marion, Geoff, Hélène, and so many others I met and walked with

- My nephew Jason Klinck who supported, encouraged, and believed in the book

- Janet Poyen who patiently and tenaciously worked through editing

- Friends in Calgary writers' circles and many others in Australia and in France whose support made such a difference

- Charlene Dobmeier, for her guidance

ABOUT
THE AUTHOR

P atricia Klinck grew up in the shadow of the Canadian Rockies. A deep love of languages (she is fluent in English, French, and Spanish) and other cultures prompted her to travel and study widely. Her professional background includes faculty positions at the University of Calgary, visiting faculty terms at Melbourne University, Edith Cowan University, and senior leadership positions at the Calgary Board of Education and St. Albert Public Schools. Since 1996, she has managed her own company, KeyLinks International Consulting Ltd., in Canada and Australia, working with innovative approaches and programs in leadership. She currently lives in Calgary, Alberta.

Website: www.keylinks.ab.ca
Blog: patklinck.wordpress.com